REPTILES

Explore the Fascinating Worlds of . . .

ALLIGATORS AND CROCODILES
LIZARDS
SNAKES
TURTLES

by Deborah Dennard
Illustrations by Jennifer Owings Dewey

NorthWord Press
Chanhassen, Minnesota

Photography © 2004: Deborah Dennard: p. 77; Michael H. Francis: pp. 9, 52, 56-57, 70, 112, 120-121, 137, 149, 158, 162; James E. Gerholdt: pp. 124-125, 134, 156-157; Saul Gonor/Seapics.com: pp. 22-23; Howard Hall/Seapics.com: p. 74; Mako Hirose/Seapics.com: p. 145; Rose Isaacs/Seapics.com: pp. 14-15; Brian Kenney: cover, pp. 4, 20, 36, 38-39, 58, 61, 64-65, 72-73, 80-81, 82, 84, 92, 96, 98, 99, 101, 104-105, 106, 110, 113, 118, 122, 130, 142, 165, 168, 176, 178-179, 181; Kitchin & Hurst/Tom Stack & Associates: p. 171; Thomas Kitchin/Tom Stack & Associates: p. 79; Gary Kramer/garykramer.net: pp. 19, 40; Wayne Lynch: pp. 16, 33, 41, 44, 46, 166-167; Joe McDonald/Tom Stack & Associates: p. 102; Gary Milburn/Tom Stack & Associates: p. 10; Robert & Linda Mitchell: pp. 53, 54, 85, 91, 132-133; Carlos Navarro/Seapics.com: p. 35; Mark Newman/Tom Stack & Associates: p. 150; Mike Parry/Tom Stack & Associates: pp. 12, 29, 30; Doug Perrine/Seapics.com: pp. 7, 24, 161, 172-173, 174, 177, 184; Ed Reschke: pp. 114-115, 154; Allen Blake Sheldon: pp. 42-43, 62, 67, 117, 123, 127, 128, 129, 138, 144, 146, 152-153, 159; Barry Silkstone: pp. 86-87, 88; Tom & Therisa Stack/Tom Stack & Associates: p. 6; Masa Ushioda/Seapics.com: pp. 26-27; Dave Watt/Tom Stack & Associates: pp. 50, 90; James D. Watt/Seapics.com: pp. 68-69.

Illustrations by Jennifer Owings Dewey

NorthWord Press
18705 Lake Drive East
Chanhassen, MN 55317
1-800-328-3895
www.northwordpress.com

Library of Congress Cataloging-in-Publication Data
Dennard, Deborah.
   Reptiles / by Deborah Dennard ; illustrated by Jennifer Owings Dewey.
      p. cm. – (Our wild world)
   Summary: Describes the physical characteristics, habits, and natural environment of various species of alligators, crocodiles, lizards, snakes, and turtles from around the world.
   ISBN 1-55971-880-3 (hardcover)
     1. Reptiles–Juvenile literature. [1. Reptiles] I. Dewey, Jennifer, ill. II. Title. III. Our wild world series.

QL644.2.D46 2004
597.9–dc21
                                   2003044568

Printed in Malaysia   10 9 8 7 6 5 4 3 2 1

REPTILES

TABLE OF CONTENTS

Explore the Fascinating World of . . .

Alligators and Crocodiles

ALLIGATORS and crocodiles have been around since the time of the dinosaurs. In ancient times they looked very much like alligators and crocodiles do today. Even with their long history, these amazing creatures remain a mystery to people.

Alligators and crocodiles are reptiles, like snakes, lizards, and turtles. All reptiles have dry, scaly skin. Alligators and crocodiles have special scales. They are like suits of armor, with thick, tough plates that protect them.

Crocs open their mouths to display and to help cool off their bodies when they get too warm.

American alligators are found in shallow pools of fresh water through much of the southern part of the United States.

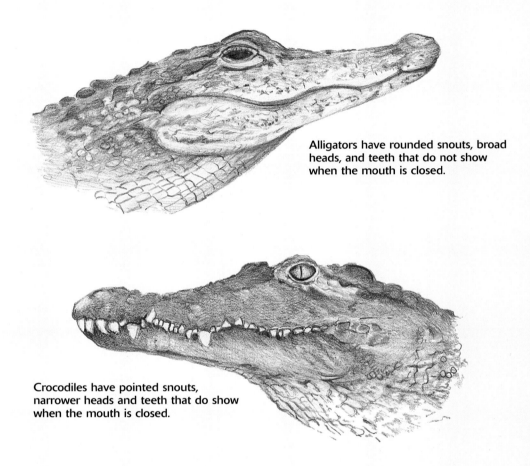

Alligators have rounded snouts, broad heads, and teeth that do not show when the mouth is closed.

Crocodiles have pointed snouts, narrower heads and teeth that do show when the mouth is closed.

Alligators, crocodiles, and all other reptiles are cold-blooded. This means that their body temperature is the same as the air or water around them. Reptiles control their body temperature by sitting in the sun to get warm or by sitting in the shade or the water to cool off. Alligators and crocodiles sometimes sit in the sun with their mouths held open. This probably helps them to cool their heads as they warm their bodies.

Alligators and crocodiles are very

The very rare American crocodile is found only in extreme southern Florida and some islands in the Caribbean.

similar, but there are some differences. Alligators have a rounded mouth and snout, or nose, and a broad head. Crocodiles have a triangular-shaped head and a pointy snout and mouth. Some crocodiles have a large tooth in the bottom jaw near the front that can be seen when their mouths are closed. On other crocodiles, many teeth show. Alligators do not show their teeeth when their mouths are closed. Crocodile eyes are a bit smaller and closer together than alligator eyes. This makes crocodiles appear to be cross-eyed.

Black caimans are related to alligators and live in Central and South America.
They are prized for their fine black hides.

There are only about 23 different kinds, or species (SPEE-sees), of alligators and crocodiles in the world. Ten of these are alligators or caimans (CAY-muns), which are very similar. Thirteen of these species are crocodiles. As a group scientists call them all crocodilians (croc-uh-DILL-ee-uns). Sometimes they call them crocs for short.

Most crocodilians cannot survive in extreme temperatures. Most do not live in places where the temperature freezes. They do not live where the weather is too hot and dry. Crocodilians dig down into the ground for protection (pro-TEK-shun) from heat and drought (DROWT). A drought is a long stretch of time without rain. Crocs dig shallow holes where water and mud collect, called mud wallows or gator holes. Mud and water may stay in these gator holes long after other areas are dry. The mud and water help to keep crocodilians from overheating.

Crocodilian FUNFACT:

Crocodilian hearts beat as slowly as 5 beats per minute in cool water, 50 degrees Fahrenheit (10 Celsius). They beat as quickly as 45 beats per minute in warm water, 82 degrees Fahrenheit (28 Celsius).

This Australian saltwater crocodile was found swimming in the ocean at the Great Barrier Reef.

Water is important to all crocodilians. They live in or near rivers, lakes, streams, ponds, pools, marshes, and swamps. The saltwater crocodile from Australia lives in salt water in the ocean, both near shore and in open waters.

Alligators and crocodiles spend most of their lives in the water. Their flat tails act as powerful flippers. Their tails steer them through the water quickly and quietly by swishing back and forth in a pattern that looks like the letter "S." Crocodilians' feet are held next to the body when they swim. Their feet paddle slowly to tread water when they float.

When a crocodilian treads water, only its eyes and nostrils are visible. The rest of its body is hidden just below the surface. With its nostrils just above the water a crocodilian can breathe air. With its eyes just peeking above the water it can watch for danger and dinner.

Crocodilians grow new teeth throughout their lives. As the old teeth break or become dull, they fall out and are replaced by new teeth. Crocodilians can have hundreds, even thousands, of teeth in their lifetime.

Crocodilians have different scales on different parts of their bodies.
Some are thick and spiky for protection.
Others are smaller and thinner for easier movement.

Alligators and crocodiles have scales of all different shapes and sizes on their bodies. The scaly skin on the head is very strong and tight and made of different shapes, like a quilt. The scales on the back are very hard and usually have a raised ridge for protection. Scales on the legs are shaped like diamonds or circles. Scales on the belly are nearly square.

Each type of scale is specially suited to each part of the body. For example, the square belly scales are large and smooth and make it easy to drag their bellies across the ground. The hard, ridged back scales give excellent protection. The small, circular scales on the legs are flexible for moving.

13

Alligators and crocodiles do not have lips. They cannot keep water out of their mouths. Instead, their wind pipes close up. Even their ears and nostrils shut down when they are underwater.

Crocodilians' eyes are protected from the water by an extra set of eyelids, which are so thin that crocs can see through them. These eyelids do not move up and down. They move from side to side across the eyes. Crocs automatically (ah-toe-MAT-ik-lee) cover their eyes with these extra eyelids when underwater. The eyelids work like swimming goggles and help them to see underwater.

Crocodilian
FUNFACT:

Alligators and crocodiles store fat in their bodies and can live as long as 1 or 2 years without eating.

When underwater, crocodilian eyes are protected by extra, see-through eyelids.

This caiman can move rapidly on land or swim swiftly in the water.

Alligators and crocodiles can hold their breath underwater for as long as 6 hours. They can do this because of the special way their hearts are built. Their hearts are divided into 4 parts, or chambers. All other reptiles have hearts with only 3 chambers. Alligators and crocodiles sit very still underwater and live with very little oxygen (AWK-zih-jin). Even when they are above water, they breathe very slowly, as little as 3 breaths per minute. People breathe about 18 times per minute at rest and more when in motion.

In water and on land, crocodilians are able to move very well. Their back feet are webbed. This helps them in swimming. Their legs and hips are flexible and jointed to help them move in many different ways. All of their muscles are very powerful.

One scientist has named 24 different ways alligators and crocodiles can move. They can walk on the bottom of a lake or river, or float and paddle at the top of the water. They can float upright in the water with only their heads held above water. They can walk in many ways on land, from dragging their bodies slowly to galloping quickly like a horse.

Crocodilian
FUNFACT:

Crocs have been seen running or galloping on land as fast as 26 miles (42 kilometers) per hour for short sprints.

Alligators and crocodiles are carnivores (KAR-nuh-vorz). That means they eat meat. They get their food by hunting and killing other animals, or prey (PRAY). Crocodilians are excellent hunters. Babies and small crocs eat animals as small as snails, insects, worms, and shrimp. The larger the croc, the larger the animal it can eat.

Alligators and crocodiles with very narrow snouts eat mostly fish. Their small snouts make it easier to move in the water but harder to catch food on land. These crocs usually have needle-like teeth for catching and holding fish.

Alligators and crocodiles with wider snouts can eat larger animals and a greater variety of animals that live on land or in the water.

Most crocodilians lie in the water to wait for their prey. A croc's prey is usually caught when the prey stops to take a drink of water and does not see the hungry hunter waiting. When its prey comes close enough, a croc can move quickly. It can even jump in the air or lunge out of the water onto land. A croc will usually grab its prey and drag it underwater.

Crocodilian
FUNFACT:

The largest of all crocodilians are the saltwater crocodiles from Australia. When fully grown, they can kill water buffalo and horses.

American alligators lie in wait for their prey in shallow water.

A raccoon drinking at the water's edge has become the prey of an alligator hiding in the water.

Some crocodilians have special diets. The common caiman in South America can feed on piranha (pih-RAH-nah) fish. The sharp teeth of the piranha are not able to bite through the caimans' tough scales.

Some crocs have special ways of hunting for their prey. The African slender-snouted crocodile uses its tail to gather fish in shallow water. Then it sweeps up the fish in its jaws.

All alligators and crocodiles swallow small animals whole. Larger prey animals may take days to consume. Saltwater crocodiles push the body of a large animal such as a water buffalo up under a ledge or rock in the water. They return for many days to feast.

Nile crocodiles change their diet as they grow. Babies up to 20 inches (50 centimeters) long eat insects. Small adults up to 10 feet (3 meters) eat fish and birds. Large adults up to 16 feet (5 meters) eat large animals, like zebras.

Nile crocodiles in Africa and saltwater crocodiles in Australia may attack people who come too close to the water. That is why people must be careful when visiting the places where these wild and dangerous animals live.

Crocodilians eat stones that stay in their stomachs. Scientists believe these stones do 2 jobs. Crocs use their sharp teeth to kill prey, not to chew them into little pieces. The stones help to crush the food once it is in their stomachs. Acids in their stomachs also work to digest the food.

The weight of the swallowed stones also helps crocodilians to float just below the surface of the water. This is the same reason human divers wear weight belts. The extra weight helps keep their bodies below the water's surface.

Crocodilian
FUNFACT:

Adult crocs can eat as much as 20 percent, or one-fifth, of their total body weight in a meal. This would be like a 100-pound (45-kilogram) person eating 20 pounds (9 kilograms) of food at once!

The senses of sight, hearing, and smell are very important to alligators and crocodiles. Crocs can see in color. They can see near and far, and they can see at night and during the day. The pupils of their eyes are larger at night to allow in more light. Their pupils are smaller and slit-like during the day to keep out too much light. Their good vision helps them search for food.

Underwater, crocs cannot hear very well because their ears are closed to keep out water. Above the water they can hear the bellows, roars, moans, grunts, and other sounds that other adult crocs make. They also can hear the high-pitched sounds made by their babies. It is important for alligators and crocodiles to hear well because they are the noisiest of all of the reptiles. They use sounds to communicate.

Scientists have learned that crocodilians can sense very small vibrations (vie-BRAY-shuns) in the water with the bumps on their faces and mouths. These bumps feel the movement of even a tiny ripple in the water. They are very helpful in finding food.

The Australian freshwater crocodile is much smaller
and less aggressive than the Australian saltwater crocodile.

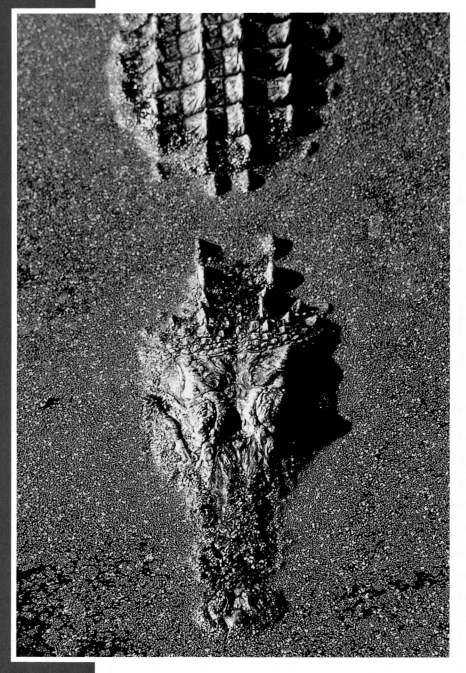

Alligator and crocodile nostrils are located on the top of the very end of their long snouts. This allows them to breathe when most of their bodies are underwater. Crocodilians also use their nostrils for their sense of smell. Scientists think crocs can recognize others by smell. Babies may even be able to smell adult males nearby. This may help them to get away safely. This is important because adult crocs sometimes eat baby crocs.

A crocodilian lying perfectly still on the bank of a river or floating in the water can look just like a log. Even their rough, scaly skin looks like the bark of a tree. This gives them very good camouflage (KAM-uh-flaj). Camouflage allows an animal to hide by blending into the surrounding water, plants, dirt, or rocks.

Tiny floating plants called duckweed help this American alligator to hide in a pool of water.

Crocodilians have very few predators (PRED-uh-torz), or animals that hunt them for food, in the wild. This is because they are so large and are very alert.

There are some dangers, though. Larger alligators and crocodiles may eat smaller ones. In South America, jaguars (JAG-wahrs) may attack crocodilian nests. Anacondas (an-uh-CON-duhs), the largest snakes in the world, may eat smaller caimans. In Australia, large lizards dig into crocodile nests to eat the eggs. In Africa, hippos, lions, and elephants have been known to kill Nile crocodiles. This is unusual and happens only if the predators are frightened or if the crocodiles threaten their babies.

Fully-grown adults sometimes may fight with each other until one of them dies. A fight to the death can happen when an alligator or crocodile is protecting its territory or home. It also can happen when a female is protecting her nest. Some scientists think that adult crocs protect nests of babies so they can eat the babies themselves. Crocs sometimes fight during mating season. They also may fight among themselves during the dry season, when water and food become scarce.

Crocodilians in the wild may live to be 40 or 50 years old. Some scientists believe that a few individuals may live much longer, as long as 70 or 80 years.

Crocs cannot fully close their mouths underwater. To keep from swallowing water, their wind pipes close when underwater.

Most crocodilian mothers give their babies some protection. Mother Nile crocodiles lead their babies around for nearly 2 years, and the youngsters obediently follow. Scientists do not believe that the mothers teach their babies anything during this time. The babies follow from instinct and are protected from danger just because their large mother is near.

Sure signs of the mating season for alligators and crocodiles are the loud noises they make. Males and females make a sound that is a lot like the roar of a lion. They use the sounds to find each other for mating. They also communicate by slapping their heads on the water or thrashing their tails in the water. With noises, crocs announce their home territories and their interest in finding a mate.

Crocodilian
FUNFACT:

Australians call saltwater crocodiles "salties" for short. They call freshwater crocodiles "freshies" for short.

Saltwater crocodiles strike with great speed and strength.
They may grab their prey and thrash around with it underwater until it is dead.

These saltwater crocodile hatchlings are leaving their eggs and their nest for the first time. Most will not survive to be 19-foot giants.

Usually the female builds the nest for her babies. Some species of alligators and crocodiles build large nests. Others build smaller nests. Some dig holes to use as nests. Some build mounds as nests. Some nests are a combination of holes and mounds.

Schneider's dwarf caimans in South America have very unusual nests. They often dig holes around the base of a large termite mound and lay their eggs there. This helps to keep the eggs warm.

American crocodiles dig a hole for a nest in a spot above the high water mark, so that the nest does not become flooded. American alligators build large mud, stick, and leaf nests above ground. These nests are so large and have been built for so many thousands of years that they have changed the land where alligators live, building up soil above water level. That is why alligators are sometimes called living bulldozers.

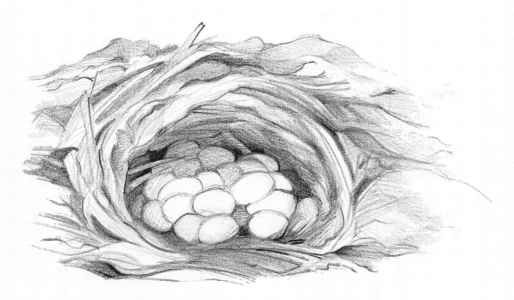

These American alligator eggs will stay warm because the decaying plants in the nest create heat.

Scientists have spent a lot of time studying the way in which American alligators build their nests. First the alligators make a path through the brush to find the right place for their nest. The nest may be 7 feet (2.1 meters) wide. It may be 42 inches (about 1 meter) high.

The nest is made of twigs, leaves, sticks, and dirt carried by the mother alligator into the nest. Females build their nests during the night and then dig a hole in the nest. There they lay their eggs. Using their back feet they carefully place each egg safely down in the nesting hole.

Baby crocs use a bump at the end of their snouts called
an egg tooth to make their way out of their eggs.

Once the eggs are laid, the mother alligator covers them over with more leaves and sticks. She stays near the nest until the babies hatch. Her presence may help to keep the babies safe. As the leaves and dirt rot, they create heat and keep the eggs warm.

After 2 or 3 months, the eggs are ready to hatch. The babies make a little croaking sound from inside the egg that easily can be heard outside of the nest. They begin to make their way out of their eggs using a bump on the end of their noses called an egg tooth. The mother may sit by and let the babies hatch themselves. She also may open the nest with her strong jaws and sharp teeth, and gently help the babies out of their eggs. The mother even may carry the babies to the water in her mouth.

A group of baby alligators is called a pod.

The mother alligator stays near the babies for a while to protect them. Sometimes they even sit on her back. When they first hatch, the babies are about 8.5 inches (21.6 centimeters) long. By the time they are just 1 year old, they will be 24 inches (61 centimeters) long. Still, many babies are lost in the first year. Animals such as herons, snakes, wildcats, otters, turtles, skunks, raccoons, large catfish, and even other alligators may eat the babies.

Those that survive will grow to be somewhere between 6 and 12 feet (1.8 to 3.7 meters) long. There have been rare examples of extra large alligators. The largest American alligator ever measured was found in 1890. It was about 19 feet (5.8 meters) long. Alligators this large are very, very unusual.

In addition to the American alligator, there is one other main species of alligator. This is the Chinese alligator. The Chinese alligator is a rare animal found mostly around the Yangtze (YANG-see) River. Chinese alligators grow to about 6.6 feet (2 meters) long. Chinese alligators are unusual because they can live where temperatures may freeze. The only other crocodilian that can stand freezing temperatures is the American alligator.

To survive the cold, Chinese alligators dig burrows between 5 feet (1.5 meters) and 60 feet (18 meters) long. There they slow down their heartbeats and their breathing and wait until the weather becomes warmer. They may be inactive for 6 or 7 months of every year.

Crocodilian
FUNFACT:

Chinese alligators may float in icy cold
water or just below a layer of ice.
As long as their nostrils are above the ice
for breathing, they can survive.

This baby caiman shows the bony eyebrow ridges that make this croc appear to be wearing glasses.

Caimans are so closely related to alligators they are like first cousins. Their heads are not as broad as an alligator's head and not as narrow as the heads of crocodiles. Their belly scales are harder and tougher than the belly scales of any other croc in the world. For many years this made them safe from hunters because their skins were too hard to tan into leather. New ways have been found to soften their hides though, so now they also are hunted for their skins.

Caimans live in Central and South America. They get their food by drowning and crushing their prey. Then they stick their heads straight up out of the water to swallow with a gulp.

They use their back legs and feet differently than any other alligator or crocodile. Like a dog, they rub their eyes and scratch themselves with their back legs. They even hold on to food with their back legs as they tear it into pieces with their powerful jaws.

Caimans are like alligators because of the shape of their rounded snout and their teeth, which are hidden when their mouths are closed. Most caimans are smaller than alligators.

There are 8 species of caimans. The smallest is the dwarf caiman that lives around the Amazon and Orinoco Rivers in South America. It grows to be only about 5 feet (1.5 meters) long. In fact, this is the smallest of any alligator or crocodile in the world.

The largest of all of the caimans is the black caiman that lives in quiet rivers and grassy wetlands in Peru, Ecuador, and Colombia. It grows to be 19.7 feet (6 meters) long.

The beautiful color of the black caiman's skin is the main reason it is an endangered (en-DANE-jurd) animal. It is a rich, dark shade of black. Hunters kill these animals to sell their skins. The skins are made into purses, boots, shoes, and wallets. Even though there are laws to protect the black caimans, many are still killed illegally. Without the protection of people, they may become extinct (ex-TINKD). This would mean that there would be none left in the world.

Common caimans are not endangered. There may be as many as 4 million in Venezuela. There are enough caimans in Venezuela to allow some hunting.

Crocodilian
FUNFACT:

Another name for the common caiman
is the spectacled caiman. Bony ridges around
the eyes make them look like they are
wearing glasses, or spectacles.

The American crocodile lives from the very tip of the state of Florida down into Central and South America and even on a few Caribbean Islands.

American crocodiles like to live in brackish water, or water that is slightly salty. Brackish water is found where the fresh water of lakes and rivers meets the salt water of oceans. These places are called estuaries (ESS-chew-air-eez).

American crocodiles eat mostly fish and grow to be about 13 feet (4 meters) long. People seldom see them because they are shy and move only at night. They also are very rare. About 10 years ago scientists estimated that no more than 500 American crocodiles were alive in Florida.

American crocodiles have learned to adapt to change. South of Miami, Florida, a colony, or group, of these crocs moved into manmade water canals built outside a power plant. The crocodiles build nests on dams made by people to hold water. Workers have seen female American crocodiles take mouthfuls of sand from a construction site to carry to their nests.

Temperature is important to these baby American crocodiles before they hatch. The eggs hatch males if the temperature of the nest is warm. The eggs hatch females if the nest is cooler.

In Africa, Nile crocodiles are strong and fierce hunters that grow to be 16.4 feet (5 meters) long. They can be found in large numbers in lakes and rivers. They eat fish. They also lie in wait for large mammals to come and drink the water. Nile crocodiles can kill animals as large as antelope, giraffes, zebras, lions, young hippos, and buffalo. They also eat carrion (KARE-ee-un), or animals that are already dead. Sometimes they gather in groups of over 100 to gorge themselves on carrion.

These fierce crocs are also dangerous to people. Records show that Nile crocodiles kill more people every year than all of the other dangerous animals in Africa combined.

Nile crocodiles are some of the most dangerous animals in all of Africa.

This saltwater crocodile shows only the large bottom tooth. Other crocodile species show many teeth.

Australian saltwater crocodiles are the largest of all crocodilians. They can grow to be 19.7 feet (6 meters) long. They can weigh as much as 2,420 pounds (1,089 kilograms). The name can be confusing, though, because these crocodiles can be found in all types of water, not just salt water. They can be found in fresh water, brackish water, and salt water. They even can be found in the open oceans and have been tracked traveling as far as 688 miles (1,100 kilometers) through ocean waters.

As saltwater crocodiles grow, their diet changes. Until they are about 6.5 feet (2 meters) long, saltwater crocodiles eat fish, crabs, and turtles. Once they are bigger they hunt for larger fish, snakes, large water birds such as herons, and dingoes, which are Australian wild dogs. The largest of the saltwater crocs can attack and eat kangaroos, horses, wild pigs, and even water buffalo.

Freshwater crocodiles are found in the northern parts of Australia in rivers, streams, and ponds called billabongs. At just 6.5 feet (2 meters) long, freshwater crocodiles are much smaller than saltwater crocodiles and do not harm people. When they are young, they eat small animals, such as fish, insects, and spiders. As they grow they catch and eat water birds, lizards, and even wallabies, which are related to kangaroos.

Many of the native Australian people, or Aborigines (ab-uh-RIJ-uh-nees), believe that crocodiles are sacred animals. One belief is that all of Australia began as a crocodile. Another belief is that people owe their lives to a spirit called the Great Crocodile.

Crocodilian
FUNFACT:

Ancient Egyptians believed that Nile crocodiles were sacred, or holy. They even made thousands of crocodile mummies.

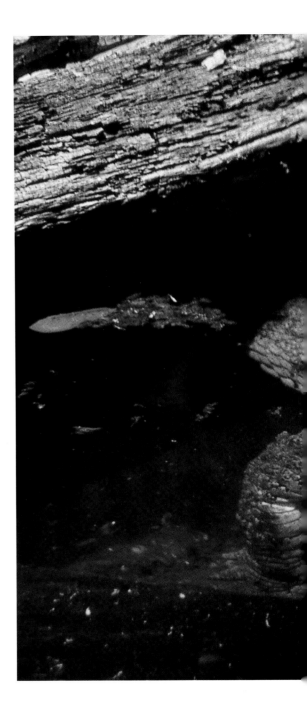

This grown freshwater crocodile now eats birds, snakes, lizards, and even wallabies.

Gharials have more than 100 teeth.

Gharials (GAR-ee-als), or gavials (GAV-ee-als), may be the most unusual of all crocodilians. Their legs are so small and weak that on land they are only able to slide their bodies slowly along. Unless they are warming themselves in the sun or laying their eggs, they stay in the water.

Gharials find their food in the water. They eat fish and frogs. They catch them by slashing their long, skinny, pointed snouts back and forth in the water. Their long snouts are well suited to catching prey in the water but not on land.

Gharials have more than 100 razor-sharp teeth. Males also have a large, ball-like bump on the end of their snouts. They live in rivers in the northern part of India and in Nepal, Pakistan, and Bangladesh. Some scientists think that gharials are a type of crocodile. Others think they are a completely different type of crocodilian and not a type of alligator or crocodile at all.

Alligators and crocodiles are strong and fierce hunters that are perfectly suited to the swamps, rivers, and waters where they live. They are some of the most specialized animals in the world. Much mystery surrounds these reptiles and much has yet to be learned. Crocodilians are ancient animals that managed to survive when the dinosaurs did not.

Crocodilian
FUNFACT:

Crocodilian fossils, ancient bones turned into rocks over time, show that these animals have not changed much since the time of the dinosaurs, about 65 million years ago.

This baby American alligator is too small to pose any threat to the turtle on which it sits. When it is full-grown, it could make a meal of the turtle.

In the past, many alligators and crocodiles were killed because people were afraid of them. Many more were killed to make belts and shoes and wallets from their skin. Yet today it may be their hides that help to save them. Many alligators and crocodiles are now raised on farms so their skins can be harvested. This helps crocs in the wild to survive. When people raise these reptiles for their skin and meat, they do not go into the wild to hunt them.

In most places it is against the law to hunt alligators and crocodiles. Laws have been passed to protect them.

Many of these animals are endangered because people have used their wet, swampy homes to make cities and farms. The areas where alligators and crocodiles live must remain swamps in order for these ancient reptiles to survive. People can help. Because of people, American alligators and Australian saltwater crocodiles are now thriving.

The more that scientists can learn about all crocodilians, the more people will be able to help them. With some work and caring, the world can be a place for people, alligators, and crocodiles, too.

My REPTILES Adventures

The date of my adventure: _____

The people who came with me: _____

_____

Where I went: _____

What reptiles I saw:

_____   _____

_____   _____

_____   _____

_____   _____

The date of my adventure: _____

The people who came with me: _____

_____

Where I went: _____

What reptiles I saw:

_____   _____

_____   _____

_____   _____

_____   _____

My REPTILES Adventures

The date of my adventure: _____

The people who came with me: _____

_____

Where I went: _____

What reptiles I saw:

_____   _____

_____   _____

_____   _____

_____   _____

The date of my adventure: _____

The people who came with me: _____

_____

Where I went: _____

What reptiles I saw:

_____   _____

_____   _____

_____   _____

_____   _____

Explore the Fascinating World of . . .

Lizards

WHAT DO YOU THINK of when you picture a lizard? A small brown or green creature? Actually, there are about 4,000 species (SPEE-sees), or kinds, of lizards in the world. They range in size from tiny 1-inch (2.5-centimeter) geckos to giant Komodo (kuh-MOE-doe) dragons up to 10 feet (3 meters) long. Lizards can be nearly any color of the rainbow. They live in many different habitats, from tropical rain forests to deserts.

Lizards are part of a group that scientists call *Class Reptilia*. Lizards are reptiles. Snakes, turtles, tortoises, crocodiles, and alligators are also reptiles.

Common iguanas are among the best-known of all lizards because they are often kept as pets.

Mediterranean geckos now live in parts of North America after accidentally being shipped on boats from their homes in the Mediterranean.

Lizards such as this green anole shed their skin in patches. Sometimes they eat their shed skins.

Reptiles are cold-blooded animals. This means that their bodies are the same temperature as the air or water around them. When they get cold or chilled, reptiles move into the sun to warm themselves. When they are too warm, they move into the shade to cool down. This helps reptiles make sure their bodies are not too hot or too cold.

Reptiles breathe air. Unlike amphibians, which start life with gills to breathe underwater, reptiles always need air to breathe.

Reptiles have dry, scaly skin. Their scales are like armor, or a protective cover, for their skin. As a reptile grows, its old skin becomes too small and must be shed. Underneath is a new, larger skin. In this way, lizards are similar to snakes. Snakes shed their skin, too. Snakes shed their skin all at once, while lizards shed their skin in patches. This is similar to a person with a bad sunburn. The skin comes off a little at a time.

Lizards are more like snakes than any other reptiles. They are so much alike they both belong to what scientists call *Order Squamata* (skwa-MAH-tah), a sub-group of *Class Reptilia*. In Latin, the word "squamata" means "having scales." Lizards and snakes both have scales.

It is not always easy to tell the difference between lizards and snakes. Most lizards have legs, but some do not. Most snakes do not have legs, but some do. Some pythons have tiny legs too small to be used for walking.

There are ways to tell the difference between lizards and snakes: the ears and the eyes. Lizards have ear openings, or holes in the sides of their heads for hearing sounds. Snakes do not have ear openings. They do not hear sound. Instead, they feel vibrations (vie-BRAY-shuns) through the ground.

Lizards have movable eyelids, so lizards can blink. Snakes do not have movable eyelids and cannot blink. Instead snakes' eyes are covered with see-through scales.

Lizards
FUNFACT:

The Australian thorny devil is a lizard that eats only 1 species of ant and may eat as many as 2,500 ants at a time.

Legless lizards look more like snakes or worms than like other lizards. They burrow, or crawl, underground. They are called snake lizards, glass lizards, or blind lizards. They are called blind lizards because they have poor vision. When they are underground, they do not need to see to get around or to find food. They use their sense of smell instead.

Different lizards eat different foods. Some lizards eat plants and animals. Some eat only plants. Some eat only animals. Some eat only certain types of plants or animals. Some lizards eat other lizards, insects, worms, snails, scorpions, eggs, fruit, seeds, leaves, flowers, cactus pads, and even seaweed. Smaller lizards usually eat insects. Larger lizards eat either plants or a combination of plants and animals.

Eastern glass lizards have no legs and look more like
snakes or worms than lizards.

Many lizards eat plants. This common iguana is eating a leaf.

Lizards that eat insects must be able to see well and move quickly to capture their food, or prey (PRAY). They may wait on a tree trunk or on the side of a building near a light where insects are found. Others may wait near an ant bed or climb where flowers bloom. When catching their food, lizards usually just grab and swallow their prey. Larger prey may be shaken, bashed against a rock, or turned around and swallowed headfirst.

Monitor lizards are large and aggressive. They use their powerful claws to tear apart crocodile and turtle nests so that they can eat the eggs inside. Anoles (a-NOLLS) are much smaller lizards, about 6 inches (15 centimeters) long. These lizards swim into streams and ponds to eat mosquito larvae (LAR-vee) floating on the water.

Lizards that eat plants do not have special ways to catch their food. They use their sense of smell and sense of taste to find ripe fruits, plump seeds, or green leaves.

Lizards
FUNFACT:

The Galapagos Island land iguana eats the pads and fruits of the prickly pear cactus. It chews up the pads and fruits but spits out the sticky spines of the plant.

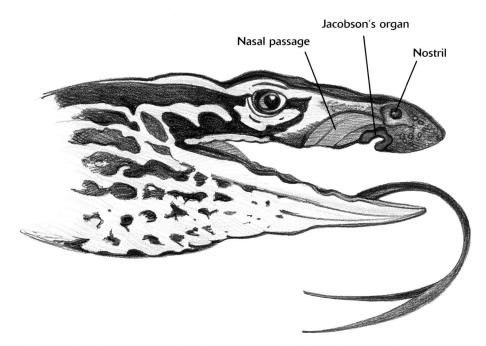

Nasal passage

Jacobson's organ

Nostril

The Jacobson's organ and related body parts are highlighted in color above.

Like snakes, many lizards have forked (FORKT) tongues. Forked tongues have a split down the middle. Lizards flick their tongues to pick up particles (PAR-tik-uls) of air and place them inside 2 holes in the roof of the mouth. These holes are called the Jacobson's organ (JAY-cub-sunz OR-gen). They allow the lizard to smell and taste the air at the same time.

The sense of sight is important to lizards. Lizards can see better than any other kind of reptile. They also can see in color. Not all animals see color. Seeing in color is important to lizards. Displaying colors to other lizards helps show where the boundaries of their territories are. Lizards also use their colors to attract a mate. Male lizards are usually more colorful than female lizards.

Basilisk lizards have crowns, bumps, or frills on their heads.

Lizards have many ways of protecting themselves. Their coloring allows them to blend in with their surroundings. This type of protection (pro-TEK-shun) is called camouflage (KAM-uh-flaj). A lizard that is camouflaged may look like the leaves, flowers, or tree bark where it lives.

Horned lizards are a good example of camouflage. Horned lizards are sometimes called horned toads. This is because of the round and flat toadlike shape of the horned lizard's body. These unusual lizards are found mostly in the dry, grassy, or desert areas of the American Southwest and in Mexico. When the sun is too hot, they bury themselves in the sand or dirt. Once they are buried, they have excellent camouflage.

This green anole has turned brown for better camouflage on the trunk of a tree.

When they are frightened, horned lizards can squirt blood at an enemy.

The way animals protect themselves is called defense. Some lizards protect themselves with thick, spiny scales that point backward. This makes them hard for a predator (PRED-uh-tor) to swallow. A predator is an animal that hunts other animals for food. If a snake or hawk catches a horned lizard, it can find itself in trouble. The sharp spines can cause serious injury if they are swallowed.

When horned lizards are frightened, they inflate their bodies with air and bounce up and down on their bellies like a ball. This confuses a predator and can save the horned lizard from being eaten.

When all other methods of defense fail, horned lizards squirt blood from their eye sockets. The blood can shoot as far as 4 feet (1.2 meters) and can be aimed in different directions.

One of the most unusual methods of defense for many lizards is the ability to lose a tail. Sometimes this happens when a predator grabs a lizard by the tail. Sometimes this happens when a lizard is frightened, even if no real danger is near. All geckos and skinks and many other lizards can drop a part of their tail. The break happens at just the right spot so there is little bleeding. Then the broken tail wiggles to distract a predator while the rest of the lizard runs away. Some lizards drop their tails often. Others only drop their tail when they need to escape. A new tail starts to grow right away.

Lizards
FUNFACT:

The 2-toed desert skink has no front legs, only 2 back legs. Each foot has only 2 toes, but they help this skink to swim through desert sands.

This gold dust day gecko is one of many lizards
that can lose a tail and then grow it back.

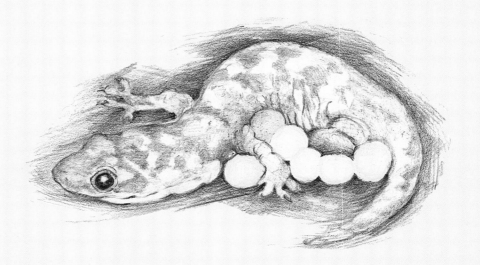

Eumeces skinks are unusual because they take care of their eggs.

Most lizards have babies at only certain times of the year. This may have to do with the climate, amount of rainfall, or when a lizard hibernates, or sleeps through part of the year.

Some lizards lay eggs. Some lizards' eggs have hard shells, like chicken eggs. Some are tough, like leather or plastic.

All eggs have to be laid in a place that is not too wet, too dry, too hot, or too cold.

Most mother lizards lay their eggs and then leave them. A few do not. Some North American skinks called Eumeces (you-ME-sees) curl their bodies around their eggs to keep them warm and safe. They may even move their

Five-lined skinks and many other lizards have leathery eggs. Babies inside must tear their way out.

eggs from one spot to another to keep them safe from danger.

Some lizards give birth to live born babies. Some have babies only once a year or once every 2 years. Some may have babies 3 or 4 times a year.

Before baby lizards can be hatched or born, the male and female lizards must find each other. This is called courtship. Many lizards have a long courtship. The males are often larger and more colorful than the females. Sometimes the males must display or even fight to win a mate.

Jackson's chameleons (kah-MEE-lee-uns) have spiny horns on their heads. The males may lock their horns and push to move another chameleon out of its tree, especially when it is looking for a mate.

Anoles fan out their baggy throats, called dewlaps (DOO-laps), to show off for a mate. Some Iguanids (ih-GWA-nids) have brightly colored undersides that they display by raising themselves up on their legs or even on their toes. They may do push-ups to flash their bright underside over and over again. They also bob their heads up and down and back and forth to show off. These mating displays often take place on top of a rock or other place where the lizards are easy to see.

When babies are hatched, they are on their own. Small species of lizards are full-grown in a matter of months. Large species, such as Komodo dragons, take years to mature. The life span of a lizard varies from a few months to perhaps as many as 20 years, depending on size and species. In general, lizards are solitary, or live alone, most of their lifetimes.

Jackson's chameleons have special 2-toed feet for climbing in trees.
Their tails can also curl around tree branches for support.

Horned lizards get their name from the spiky or horny-looking scales that protect their bodies.

One of the largest groups of lizards is called Iguanids. Iguanas, horned lizards, and many other lizards belong to this group. Iguanids can be large or small. Some have bright colors. Others are able to camouflage themselves easily. Some, like the basilisk lizard, have crests, crowns, spines, and spikes.

Some Iguanids live in trees. Others live on the ground. One species, the marine iguana, even lives part of the time in the ocean. Iguanids live mostly in North and South America. Some are scattered on the islands of Fiji, Tonga, Madagascar, the West Indies, and the Galapagos Islands.

The common, or green, iguana is a familiar Iguanid because it is often kept as a pet. This can become a problem before too long, because this iguana can grow to be as long as 6.5 feet (about 2 meters). Common iguanas have a large ragged crest on their backs and a floppy dewlap on their necks.

In Central and South America, common iguanas live near lakes, streams, and rivers. They climb to the tops of tall trees to watch over their territory. High in the treetops the males communicate by bobbing their heads up and down. This is a type of lizard warning system. The warning tells other males to stay away.

Female iguanas lay eggs in sandy soil, and the babies are about 8 inches (20 centimeters) long when first hatched. Common iguanas eat mostly plants. This is unusual because many Iguanids eat insects.

Lizards
FUNFACT:

Some lizards, such as water dragons, are very good swimmers and can hold their breath underwater for as long as 30 minutes.

Some Iguanids are extremely colorful. Common iguanas can be grass-green, blue-green, orange, or brown. The collared lizards of the desert in the American Southwest are also colorful. The male is green, black, and orange with a bright yellow band like a collar around his neck. The female is also brightly colored during mating time. That is when she turns from slate gray to brick red. When these lizards are frightened, they run on their back legs. They also can hop and jump from one rock to another in their desert home.

Lizards
FUNFACT:

The anole changes color from brown to green and is sometimes called a chameleon, but it is not. It is an Iguanid.

This green anole is the same color as the cactus on which it rests.
When on a tree trunk, it can turn brown.

Marine iguanas are medium-sized lizards, growing to be about 3 feet (0.9 meters) long.

Marine iguanas are unusual and rare lizards that can deal with both cold and hot temperatures. They live on the Galapagos Islands where the sun shines brightly and the air is warm. To get their food, they dive into the cold waters of the Pacific Ocean to graze on seaweed. To keep from getting too cold in the water, their hearts beat only half as fast in the water as on land. This makes their blood move slowly and not chill too quickly. When they return to land, their hearts speed up again, their blood moves faster, and their bodies warm up quickly.

When they are underwater, marine iguanas use their flat tails to steer themselves. They hold their breath for a long time, even as they feed. When returning to their dry, island homes, the females and young climb on top of each other in large piles to lie in the sun and warm themselves. The males spread themselves around, careful not to get too close to other males. By staying away from each other, the males are less likely to fight.

Lizards
FUNFACT:

Marine iguanas have glands in their nostrils to filter out the salt in the seawater. They get rid of the extra salt by sneezing it out.

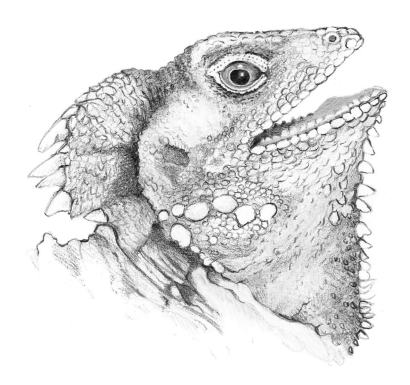

Agamids may have extra flaps of skin that look like crests or crowns on their heads and frills or hoods around their necks.

Agamid (ah-GAH-mid) lizards are similar to Iguanids, but Agamids come mostly from the Old World continents of Asia, Australia, and Africa. Iguanids come mostly from the New World, which includes North and South America.

Another difference between Agamids and Iguanids is the way their teeth are set. Iguanid teeth are set in deep sockets in their jawbones. Agamid teeth are set just along the upper edge of the jaw.

All Agamids lay eggs, and they are all insect eaters. They also have short, muscular tongues.

African rainbow lizards may not have every color of the rainbow, but they do have bright shades of red, blue, and yellow.

Agamids may have extra flaps of skin that look like crests or crowns on their heads and frills or hoods around their necks. They may have spines, bright colors, or all of these things. The African rainbow lizard is one of the most beautiful Agamids. The male is brightly colored with red and blue bands. Its color becomes even brighter when he shows off to another male or to the smaller, brown-and-gray females.

During displays males bob their heads and their whole bodies to make the most of their beautiful colors. Often these beautiful lizards live near people, in yards, parks, and gardens.

Australia is the place to find 2 of the most unusual of all Agamid lizards. The frilled lizard grows to be 3 feet (0.9 meters) long. It has a large, round flap of skin all the way around its neck that can be opened like an umbrella. This can be a very effective way to scare off predators or to show off to another lizard.

The frilled lizard also can open its mouth to show the bright orange inside, and it hisses when frightened. If that is not enough to scare away a predator, it can even rise up on its back legs and run. The frilled lizard spends most of its time in the trees, and only displays on the ground.

A cousin to the frilled lizard is the bearded lizard, which has a sharp spiny beard along its chin. It lives mostly on the ground in the dry, scrubby parts of Australia. The bearded lizard opens its bright yellow mouth when it is alarmed.

Lizards
FUNFACT:

Draco (DRAY-ko) lizards, also called flying lizards, are Agamids that can spread out flaps of skin between their ribs to show off and to glide from tree to tree.

Chameleons belong to another group of lizards. There are about 85 species of chameleons. They come from Africa, Madagascar, Asia, and the area around Sicily and Greece in southern Europe. Their bodies are flatter and less tube-shaped than those of most other lizards. This shape helps them climb in trees and look like leaves for camouflage. Their tails are prehensile (pre-HEN-sill). A prehensile tail allows chameleons to hold onto a tree branch with just the tip of the tail curled around it. When their tails are not wrapped around a tree branch, they are curled up like a spring.

This Jackson's chameleon holds onto a tree branch with its prehensile tail.

Chameleons have 2 large toes on each foot for climbing and gripping. They may have bright colors that can change. Many of them have large, oddly shaped skulls that make their heads look like they are topped with domes or caps or horns. Each eye can move in a different direction from the other. That means chameleons can look left and right or ahead of them and behind them at the same time.

Chameleons' tongues are sticky and are as long as their whole bodies. They can unroll their long tongues and catch many insects quickly. Chameleons move slowly and spend most of their lives alone. When they spot other chameleons, they hiss and open their mouths, puff their bodies up, and change colors to scare the other chameleons away. Chameleons are well known for their ability to change color. They most commonly go from speckled shades of brown to speckled shades of yellow and green. These colors help chameleons to hide better in their forest homes.

The jeweled chameleon is named for its bright, shiny spots
of color that look like gleaming jewels.

The blue tongue of this blue-tongued skink is used to warn away other animals.

Skinks belong to a large family of about 1,000 species. They live all over the world and have large, rounded scales that are smooth to the touch. Their legs are short, but most of these lizards are fast runners.

Some skinks have legs that are so small they cannot be used for walking. Some skinks have no legs at all. Instead of walking, these skinks slither (SLIH-thur) like snakes. Skinks are not as flashy, colorful, or strange-looking as many of the other types of lizards. They are a hardy type of lizard. There are more skinks than any other kind of lizards in the world.

A typical skink is small and brown and spends most of its life hiding. It lives mostly on the ground and eats insects. It may be found in grasslands or forests, jungles, mountains, deserts, parks, or backyards.

The blue-tongued skinks from Australia are fascinating reptiles. They are about 20 inches (50 centimeters) long. They have heavy bodies, short legs, and a short, fat tail. They give birth to 1 litter of large babies just once a year. They eat everything from insects and snails to fruits and seeds.

Perhaps the most unusual thing about them is their blue tongue. When frightened, a blue-tongued skink opens its mouth and sticks out its tongue as a warning. Blue-tongued skinks are calm, quiet lizards and are sometimes kept as pets.

This mossy leaf-tail gecko has perfect camouflage and looks just like the rough bark of a tree.

Like skinks, geckos are successful lizards because they can live all over the world. There are over 800 species of geckos. They are excellent insect hunters and in many parts of the world are welcomed in people's homes as pest killers. They can climb on smooth surfaces and even up walls, glass windows, and doors. They use tiny, hairy hooks on the pads of their feet to climb this way.

Most geckos hunt only at night. They have large eyes for seeing well in the dark. Unlike most lizards, they do not have movable eyelids. Instead, each eye is covered with a large, see-through scale so that they do not miss seeing anything.

Many female geckos lay only 2 eggs, and those eggs are in shells that are as hard as bird eggshells. Geckos are unusual in this way. Most lizard species lay more eggs, and most of those eggs have tough, leathery shells. Some geckos have brightly colored skin. Others have good camouflage colors.

Tokay geckos are named for the noise they make that sounds like "Toe Kay! Toe Kay!"

A gecko that many people may know is the Mediterranean gecko. It no longer lives just in its original home in India, Iran, and North Africa. It has stowed away on ships in crates and cargoes for many years and now finds homes from Florida to Texas, as well as Mexico and Cuba.

Mediterranean geckos are only about 4 to 5 inches (10 to 12 centimeters) long. They have brown, gray, and black splotches, and wart-like bumps on their bodies. Like other geckos, they have very large eyes and large footpads and toes for climbing.

A noisy gecko is the tokay gecko. It gets its name from the loud call it makes. The call sounds like "Toe Kay! Toe Kay!" This gecko is found in Southeast Asia. They often live in people's homes. They find a little nook or cranny and defend it as their own, even hissing at people who come too near. They also are known to bite. Tokay geckos are larger and more colorful than Mediterranean geckos. They are blue, gray, or green, with orange spots.

Monitors are some of the largest and most aggressive of all lizards. They have long bodies and tails, long necks and claws, and loose skin that hangs off their bodies like a sack. There are only 30 species of monitors, and most of these live in Australia.

The perentie (peh-RENT-tee) lives on the edges of Australian deserts and may grow to be 8 feet (2.4 meters) long. They hide behind rocks and attack and eat other reptiles, small mammals, and carrion, or dead animals. The lace monitor climbs in trees and takes birds and eggs from nests. It eats whatever small animal it can catch.

Lizards
FUNFACT:

In Australia, monitors are called goannas (go-ANN-uhs). Not all of them are large. One insect-eating goanna is only 8 inches (20 centimeters) long and is not as fierce as other goannas.

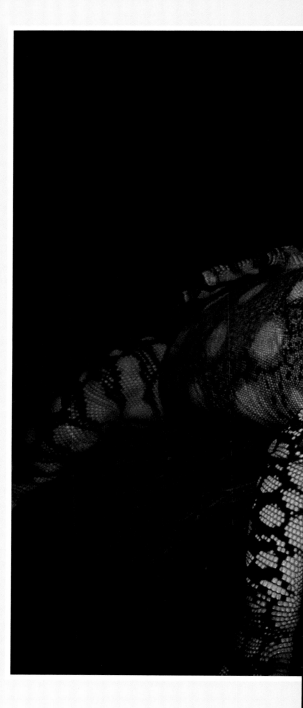

Perentie monitors from Australia are the second largest lizards in the world.

Komodo dragons are not fire-breathing dragons, but they are very large and aggressive lizards.

Lizards range in size from the 10-foot (3-meter) Komodo dragon
to tiny 1-inch (2.5-centimeter) geckos.

The largest of all lizards is the Komodo dragon, found only on Komodo Island and a few other small islands in Indonesia. They are not really dragons. They are monitor lizards. They are called dragons because they grow to be large—as long as 10 feet (3 meters) and 300 pounds (136 kilograms). Young Komodo dragons eat insects and small animals. Adults hunt pigs and deer. People come to Komodo Island to see the dragons, and they are careful not to get too close.

The Nile monitor from Africa is another large monitor. It eats eggs, including crocodile eggs. It digs up crocodile eggs from buried nests, all the time watching for the mother crocodile that may be nearby.

This Mexican beaded lizard is feasting on a bird egg taken from a nest in the desert.

Poisonous lizards are unusual. In fact there are only 2 kinds: the beaded lizards and the gila (HEE-luh) monsters. Both live in the deserts of the south-western United States and in northern Mexico. Scientists believe they are closely related to monitors.

Both types of poisonous lizards have short, stumpy tails and rounded, bead-like, bumpy scales. Beaded lizards and gila monsters have colored blotches of skin in shades of pink and black or yellow and black. They store fat in their short, thick tails. This extra fat gets them through the times when they cannot find food. Their bodies are close to the ground, and they move slowly over the desert sands.

The deserts where these poisonous lizards live can be very hot. To deal with

Gila monsters use their poison for defense. People are seldom harmed by them.

the heat, they hide underground in burrows or beneath rocks. The deserts can also be cold, even freezing. They hibernate during the coldest months. They may also hibernate during the hottest and driest parts of the year.

Food is scarce in the desert. Beaded lizards and gila monsters may not eat often. When they do, they use their sense of smell to find nesting birds, eggs, or other small animals beneath the sand. They use their legs and claws to dig down to find food.

Poisonous lizards use their poison mostly for defense. The poison is not injected through fangs as in snakes. Instead the poison seeps into a wound caused by sharp, grooved teeth bites. Their bites are not usually fatal, unless they have the chance to chew on a victim.

Western collared lizards have bright yellow and green bands around their necks, making them look like they are wearing a fancy collar.

Lizards come in many shapes, colors, and sizes. They live almost everywhere in the world, but many lizards are rare or even endangered (en-DANE-jurd). They are becoming endangered mostly because of the loss of their habitat. Land that is changed into cities, farms, and factories for people does not make a good home for most lizards.

Some of the rarest of all lizards are the ones that live on islands. There is only so much land on an island, so there may be nowhere for lizards to go if they lose their homes.

Some lizards are taken from their homes in the wild to be kept as pets. Others are killed for their skins. What can people do to help? Learning about lizards and the places where they live is the first step. It will take the help of people to protect lizards and their homes. When people share the land, water, and plants of the earth, then humans and animals, including lizards, can all have a place to live.

My REPTILES Adventures

The date of my adventure: _____

The people who came with me: _____

_____

Where I went: _____

What reptiles I saw:

_____   _____

_____   _____

_____   _____

_____   _____

The date of my adventure: _____

The people who came with me: _____

_____

Where I went: _____

What reptiles I saw:

_____   _____

_____   _____

_____   _____

_____   _____

My REPTILES Adventures

The date of my adventure: _____

The people who came with me: _____

_____

Where I went: _____

What reptiles I saw:

_____   _____

_____   _____

_____   _____

_____   _____

The date of my adventure: _____

The people who came with me: _____

_____

Where I went: _____

What reptiles I saw:

_____   _____

_____   _____

_____   _____

_____   _____

Explore the Fascinating World of . . .

Snakes

SNAKES ARE AMAZING animals. They come in a rainbow of colors. They are excellent hunters. Different snakes eat everything from ants to pigs. They live in many places in the world.

There are between 2,500 and 3,000 species (SPEE-sees), or kinds, of snakes in the world. Each species is perfectly suited for its own special habitat, or the type of place it lives. Snakes belong to a large group of animals that scientists call *Class Reptilia*. Snakes are reptiles. Reptiles are cold-blooded animals. This means that the temperature of a snake's body is the same as the air or water around it.

The bright, beautiful colors found in many snakes, such as this Honduran palm viper, give a warning to other animals to stay away.

African bush vipers come in 3 different colors: gray, orange, and yellow.

Many people think that snakes have slimy skin. They don't! All reptiles have dry, scaly skin. They have different types of scales on different parts of their bodies. The scales on the back and the sides of their bodies are usually in rows. In some species the scales may be small, smooth, and rounded. In other species the scales are sometimes rough and thick. They may even stick out from the body like armor or spikes.

Snakes often have scales on their bellies that are wide, flat, and smooth. This helps a snake drag itself along the ground. Scales on the head may be of different shapes and sizes. Some may be large and platelike. Others may be small and fine. Scientists use scale patterns along the back and sides of a snake to identify the species.

There are 4 main groups of reptiles. Snakes and lizards belong to a group called *Order Squamata* (skwa-MAH-tah). The second group of reptiles includes turtles and tortoises. The third group includes alligators and crocodiles. The fourth group is made up only of the tuatara (too-ah-TAR-ah), a reptile from New Zealand.

Snakes
FUNFACT:

The longest known snake in the United States was an indigo snake that measured just under 9 feet (2.7 meters) long.

Male indigo snakes are very territorial during mating season and have been known to use their teeth to make 6-inch (15-centimeter) long cuts on other males.

Anacondas are often found soaking in water.

Snakes do not have legs for walking. They slither (SLIH-thur) or glide instead of walk. Snakes do not have eyelids. Their eyes are covered in dry scales, just like the rest of their bodies. Snakes have long forked (FORKT) tongues. A forked tongue is split down the middle and has 2 sections.

Snakes come in many sizes and colors. Most are thin and small, less than 3 feet (0.9 meters) long. Some grow to be very long with thick, heavy bodies. The biggest snake in the world is the anaconda (an-uh-CON-duh) that may grow to be over 26 feet (7.9 meters) long.

Sidewinders loop their bodies as they move, leaving an unusual track behind.

Snakes of all sizes have flexible spines and strong muscles. When they move, they flex their muscles and stretch their spines. This makes some snakes seem to weave their way across the ground in the shape of an "S."

Flexible spines and strong muscles also allow some snakes to climb trees. Others burrow underground or fit into tiny hiding places. Snakes known as sidewinders loop one part of their bodies in the air as they move. They look like they are winding sideways across the desert sands. When other snakes move, they seem to stretch themselves out, then pull themselves together, just like the folds in an accordion.

The green mamba is a highly venomous snake related to the cobra.
Its long, slender body is perfect for slithering through the treetops.

This Gaboon viper (right) has shed its skin (left).
Even the eye scales are visible in the shell of the shed skin.

All snakes shed their skin, and they do this throughout their entire lives. As they grow their old skin becomes too small. A new, larger skin grows underneath. When the old skin is ready to be shed, a snake may rub back and forth against a rock to loosen the old skin. It may soak in water to loosen the old skin. Then the snake simply slithers out of it. Scientists can look at a skin that has been shed and identify what species of snake it is from.

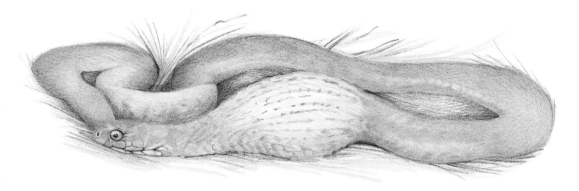

Some snakes swallow eggs whole and do not crush them
until the egg is in their stomachs.

Snakes are predators (PRED-uh-torz). Predators hunt and kill other animals for food. Even very small snakes hunt prey (PRAY), or animals for food. Very small snakes eat animals as tiny as ants, crickets, or worms. Medium-sized snakes eat rats, mice, or rabbits. Very large snakes eat animals as large as pigs or deer.

Snakes must be very good hunters in order to survive. Different snakes have different ways of hunting. Some snakes open their mouths very wide and even unhinge (un-HINJ), or separate, their jaws so they can eat things that are larger than their heads. Some snakes strike very quickly at their prey, grabbing it with their mouths and swallowing.

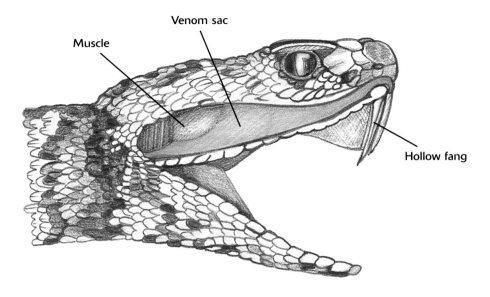

Muscle

Venom sac

Hollow fang

Venom is made and stored in large venom sacs and injected into prey through hollow teeth called fangs. These parts are highlighted in color above.

Boas, anacondas, and pythons are constrictors. Constrictors are snakes that grab their prey with their mouths and loop their bodies around the prey. Then they squeeze until the prey cannot breathe. Once the prey is dead, constrictors stop squeezing and swallow their meal whole.

Snakes do not use their teeth for chewing. They use their teeth for jabbing, grabbing, and swallowing.

Some snakes are venomous (VEN-im-us). Venom is poison that is injected through hollow teeth called fangs to kill prey. Venom is made in the body of a snake and is stored in venom sacs. Snakes such as rattlesnakes, with large amounts of venom and large venom sacs, usually have triangular-shaped heads. Snakes such as coral snakes, with small amounts of venom and small venom sacs, do not have triangular-shaped heads.

Snakes do not always need to eat every day or even every week. The larger the animal that a snake eats, the longer the snake can wait until it needs to eat again. Strong acids in a snake's stomach work to digest its food slowly. An anaconda may not eat for months after eating a large pig or deer!

Many people are afraid of venomous snakes. Many people believe that all snakes are venomous, but this is not true. Only about 250 out of 3,000 species of snakes are venomous. That is less than 10 percent of all snakes. Of these 250 venomous snake species, only about 50 of these have venom that is dangerous to people. Still, venomous snakes kill 100,000 people a year. Most of these deaths are from viper (VIE-pur) and cobra bites in the heavily populated parts of Africa and Asia. Australia is the place where the most venomous snakes live. However, fewer than 10 people per year are killed by venomous snakes there. The reason is there are not many people living in Australia.

There are different types of venom. Cobras and coral snakes have venom that poisons the central nervous system. Rattlesnakes and cottonmouths have venom that poisons the blood. Sea snake venom poisons the muscles. All venomous snakebites should be taken seriously. To be safe around all snakes, it is always best to leave them alone.

Snakes
FUNFACT:

In parts of southern Australia, 80 percent of all snakes are venomous. This means that almost any snake you see there will be venomous.

The Saharan sand viper can hide itself in the desert. It buries its body except for its eyes (to see) and its nostrils (to breathe).

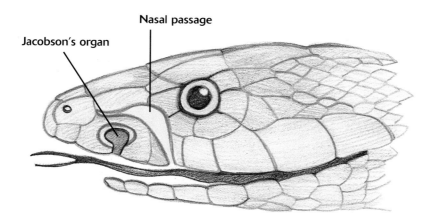

Jacobson's organ

Nasal passage

The Jacobson's organ and nasal passage are highlighted in color above.

Snakes sense the world differently than people do. Snakes do not have ear openings, so they cannot hear. Instead they feel vibrations (vie-BRAY-shuns) from the ground.

Snakes cannot blink because they do not have eyelids. Single see-through scales cover their eyes. When snakes are ready to shed their skins, the scales become foggy. Until the old skin is shed, a snake's vision is not very good. Some snakes that burrow can see very little or are completely blind. Because they spend so much time underground, these snakes do not need to see.

Probably the most important sense for a snake is a combination of taste and smell. A snake's long, forked tongue flicks out to pick up the different scents (SENTS) and flavors in the air. The tongue is then touched to 2 holes in the roof of the snake's mouth. These holes are called the Jacobson's organ (JAY-cub-sunz OR-gen). With the Jacobson's organ, snakes can both taste and smell the air all around them.

Pythons and some other snakes are able to sense heat coming from the body of a warm-blooded animal. Pits along the front edge of these snakes' mouths are very sensitive to heat. By sensing the heat, a snake may feel if a warm-blooded animal, such as a rat or a mouse, is near. This helps them find their food.

The checkered garter snake is a small, non-venomous snake that has good camouflage on the ground.

Most snakes are very good at camouflage (KAM-uh-flaj). Camouflage is the ability to blend into the surroundings to hide. Many snakes have the same colors as the rocks, plants, and dirt where they live. Brown, splotchy-colored snakes are difficult to see in leafy areas. Gray-colored snakes are hard to see in rocky areas. Green snakes are hard to see in bushes and trees.

Some snakes live in many different habitats. They may have different colors, depending on where they live. Other snakes have bright, beautiful colors as a warning that they are venomous. Their yellow, orange, and red colors warn other animals to stay away. Some snakes that are not venomous have bright warning colors. These snakes are called mimics (MIM-iks) because they copy the colors of their dangerous cousins.

Young Amazon tree boas come in 3 different colors: orange, yellow, and rust.

Some snakes change color as they grow. Emerald tree boas, for example, are yellow or red when they are babies and turn green when they are adults.

Horned vipers are the same color as the sand in the deserts where they live, but their camouflage does not end there. They wiggle their bodies into the sand until they are safely buried. The sand keeps them hidden from predators and protects them from the heat of the sun.

Copperheads are colored so that they look like dead leaves lying on the ground, a place where they often hide.

This albino hognose snake plays dead when frightened. It rolls on its back, sticks out its tongue, and even produces a foul odor.

Besides camouflage, snakes have many other ways of defending themselves. Grass snakes roll on their backs and play dead. Hognose snakes play dead and even give off a bad smell. Cobras raise their bodies off the ground and expand the muscles around their necks. This is called hooding and it sends a warning to stay away. Cobras can also spit their venom as far as 3 feet (0.9 meters) in defense. They aim for the eyes of their attacker. This would hurt but not kill the attacker.

Rattlesnakes defend themselves by making a rattling sound as a warning. Cottonmouths show the bright white inside of their mouths. Some snakes may hiss. Others puff out their bodies to look bigger and more frightening. Some snakes even rub their scales together to make a sound like scratchy sandpaper. Ball pythons roll up into a tight ball with their heads hidden in the middle for protection (pro-TEK-shun).

Some snakes live alone most of their lives, so they have to search to find a mate. They use their sense of smell and taste to find each other. Others may hibernate, or sleep through the winter, in large groups and mate when they wake up in the spring. Some of the male snakes wrestle each other for the right to mate with a female snake.

Most snakes have babies by laying eggs. These snakes must find the right place to lay their eggs. Some may lay their eggs in sand. Others lay their eggs in dirt or under rocks. The nest must be in a safe and warm place that is not too wet or too dry.

Baby snakes have a hard knob on their noses called an egg tooth. It is not a tooth at all, but a natural tool that snakes use to tear open their leathery eggs. The egg tooth falls off after the baby has hatched. Usually female snakes lay their eggs and then slither away. The babies must take care of themselves from the time they emerge from the egg.

Pythons are different. Female pythons stay with their eggs. They curl around them to keep them warm and safe. Cobras do not curl around their eggs, but they stay near their eggs to defend them.

Snakes
FUNFACT:

Puff adders may lay as many as 150 eggs at a time. Some blind snakes may lay only 1 or 2 eggs at a time.

This baby black rat snake has just begun to emerge from its shell.

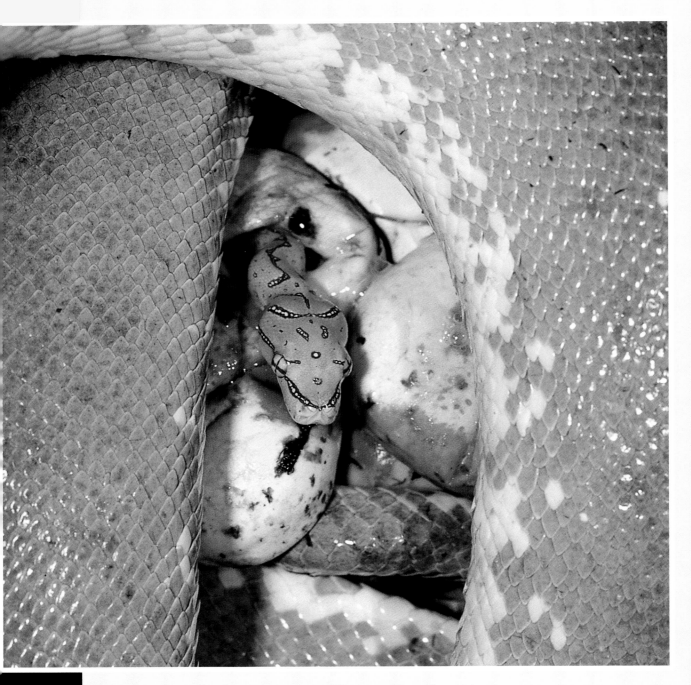

Mother green tree pythons are very unusual because they curl around
their eggs and their hatching babies.

Some snakes give birth to babies that are hatched from soft eggs held inside the mother's body. The babies are wrapped in a thin covering called a membrane. The membrane is not as thick as an eggshell. It is more like a slippery plastic bag. When a baby snake is ready to be born, it slips out of the membrane, out of its mother's body, and is out on its own.

Most water snakes have live born babies because they cannot lay their eggs in water. Most snakes that live in cold climates have live born babies because their eggs would get too cold. Most snakes that live high in trees have live born babies because they cannot lay eggs in a tree.

Snakes live in many different types of places. They live in tropical rain forests, pine forests, and oak forests. They live in swamps, in deserts, in grasslands, and on mountains. They even live where people live, from big cities to farms, ranches, parks, and backyards out in the country. Snakes are shy, though. They stay away from people whenever they can. Snakes are often present but unseen.

Snakes live underground and high in trees, in tall grass and in short grass, in bushes and in barns, underwater and on rocky hillsides. Some of the few places where snakes do not live are New Zealand and Ireland. Both of these countries are islands. This may be a clue as to why there are no snakes in these two places.

Snakes
FUNFACT:

The Martinique thread snake is perhaps the smallest of all snakes. It is about the size and shape of a pencil.

Some scientists say there are 18 groups, or families, of snakes and more than 3,000 species of snakes. Some scientists disagree and say there may only be 14 or 15 families and only about 2,400 species of snakes. No one knows for sure. That is one reason why so many people still study snakes.

No matter how many groups of snakes there are, 4 of these groups are of most interest to people.

Scientists call the largest group of snakes Colubrids (kah-LOO-brids). As many as 70 percent of all snakes may be Colubrids. These snakes are medium-sized. Their right lung is long, but their left lung is either very small or is not there at all. Their heads are covered with large scales. Colubrids may be almost any size, shape, or color. They are found all over the world in many different types of habitats. There are about 1,500 species of Colubrid snakes. Most Colubrids are not venomous, but some are. Most of the venomous Colubrids are not deadly to people.

Milk snakes are harmless snakes that look a lot like coral snakes. On milk snakes the bands of yellow touch only the bands of black.

One of the venomous snakes in Africa is the boomslang. Its long, slender body can slither gracefully through the tallest trees.

One of the venomous Colubrids is the boomslang, found in Africa. The word boomslang is an Afrikaans (af-ri-KAHNZ) word meaning tree snake. Boomslangs may be gray, black, brown, green, red, or pale blue. These colors make boomslangs hard to recognize. They have thin bodies and may be about 7 feet (2.1 meters) long. They have large eyes and live in trees and bushes where they hunt lizards, a favorite food.

Boomslangs are venomous, but their fangs are in the back of their mouths. That means to kill a lizard they must bite down for a while until the lizard is dead.

San Francisco garter snakes are brightly colored snakes that are endangered.

King snakes and milk snakes, corn snakes and rat snakes, garter snakes and hognose snakes are all Colubrids that are not venomous. Some of these are among the most colorful and most beautiful snakes in the world.

San Francisco garter snakes have bright red, blue, and black stripes. Most of their habitat is the area where the city of San Francisco now stands. Because of that, there are not many places for these snakes to live, so they are endangered (en-DANE-jurd). They are small, slender snakes that grow to be only about 2 feet (0.6 meters) long. They have large eyes. They feed mostly on fish, toads, and frogs, and they hunt mainly during the daytime.

The green anaconda is the longest snake in the world.

Boids (BOW-idz) are another group of snakes. This group includes boas and pythons, which are alike in many ways. Boids are constrictors. They are not venomous. Instead, they squeeze their prey. Most of them live in tropical parts of the world, places where it is warm all of the time.

Boas live in many parts of the world, including Central and South America. Pythons live only in Africa, Asia, and Australia. Boas hold soft eggs inside their bodies until the babies are ready to be born live into the world. Pythons lay hard-shelled eggs. The longest snakes in the world belong to the Boids group. This includes the reticulated python, Burmese python, carpet python, and the green anaconda, which is a type of boa.

Snakes
FUNFACT:

The yellow anaconda is much smaller than the green anaconda.
It grows to be only about 6 to 10 feet (about 2 to 3 meters) long.

Snakes have many ribs up and down the sides of their flexible spines.

Many Boids have 2 lungs, and many of them have tiny legs that are so small they are almost impossible to see. These legs are not large enough for walking, but they are left over from a long time ago when snakes had legs. Even their skeletons have hips bones, showing that long ago snakes had legs.

The closest relatives to snakes are lizards. Some lizards do not have legs, and some snakes, such as Boids, have tiny legs. How can snakes and lizards be told apart? Lizards have ear openings, and snakes do not.

Boids also have flexible jaws that stretch in the middle of the bottom jaw and expand at the joints. Boids can open their mouths wide and swallow whole the large prey they capture.

Some Colubrids are constrictors, such as the red milk snake.
This snake squeezes a lizard before eating it.

The rainbow boa has dark stripes on its face and head.

The rainbow boa is named for its shiny skin that seems to reflect all of the colors of the rainbow. The colors appear to change as the snake moves and as the light changes. Rainbow boas live in grasslands and in rain forests in South America. They can be found on the ground or in the trees. Young rainbow boas are more colorful than older ones. They all have large eyes and dark lines that run down the center of the head and through the eyes.

These beautiful snakes may have as many as 25 live born babies at a time. Rainbow boas eat birds and small mammals. They grow to be about 6.5 feet (about 2 meters) long.

Another beautiful snake in the Boids group comes from northern Australia and New Guinea (GIH-nee). It is called the green tree python. At just a little over 3 feet (0.9 meters) long, these are not giants at all. They only live high in the trees in the tropical rain forest where they drape, or hang, their bodies over tree branches, and they never come down to the ground. They hunt at night for roosting birds, small mammals, and reptiles. Their color gives them good camouflage.

Green tree python babies are not green. They are bright yellow. This color also gives them good camouflage by making them blend into the sunlight that shines through the leaves in the trees.

Green tree pythons are very similar to emerald tree boas in South America.

Green tree pythons can curl themselves around tree branches as soon as they are born.

This cobra is hooding, or flaring out the
sides of its neck in a display meant to scare.

The third major group of snakes is called the Elapid (eh-LAH-pid) group. Snakes in the cobra family are Elapids. Some of the most dangerous snakes in the world belong to this group, including cobras, coral snakes, sea snakes, and green mambas. Most Elapids have large fangs at the front of their mouths and can inject venom into prey very easily. All of these snakes are venomous. Their venom is very strong. They have slender bodies and large head scales.

The West African green mamba is an Elapid. Although its bite is very dangerous, it is a very shy snake that is rarely seen by people. If it is frightened, it tries to escape. It only bites if it is cornered. The green mamba has large eyes and very large greenish-yellow scales all over its body. It grows to be about 6.5 feet (about 2 meters) long and lives in the forests and woodlands of West Africa. Mambas live up in the trees and use their long, muscular bodies to travel gracefully from one branch or tree to another. This relative of the cobra is an egg-laying snake that eats rats, mice, birds, and even bats.

Snakes
FUNFACT:

When it is frightened, the harmless longnose snake buries its head in the middle of its coils and waves its red, yellow, and black banded tail. This makes it look like the head of a coral snake ready to strike.

The Texas coral snake is a much smaller cousin of the mamba and the cobras. Like the mamba, the Texas coral snake is very shy. It has venom that is 8 times stronger than the venom of any other snake in North America. This makes its venom as strong as cobra venom. However, only about 1 percent of all venomous snakebites in America come from these snakes. The reason is that they are very shy and have tiny fangs about one-eighth inch (0.3 centimeters) long.

Coral snakes have beautiful bands of red, yellow, and black. They grow to be about 2 feet (0.6 meters) long. Harmless milk snakes have the same colors, but in a different order. To tell the difference between coral snakes and milk snakes, just remember that coral snakes have bands of red touching bands of yellow. Harmless milk snakes have bands of red touching bands of black.

Coral snakes live in dry pine and oak forests and in thorny scrub, an area where there are low trees and bushes. Coral snakes hide under rocks and fallen leaves.

Venomous coral snakes have bands of red that touch bands of yellow.
That is how people can tell them from the similar-looking but harmless milk snake.

This Gaboon viper is sitting perfectly still on the floor of the forest waiting for its prey.

The last major group of snakes are the vipers. Vipers are snakes with large fangs at the front of the mouth. When they are not in use, their fangs fold back and out of the way. These special fangs can deliver a lot of venom very quickly. This makes vipers dangerous and deadly snakes.

Vipers have many small scales on their heads and heat-sensing pits between each eye and nostril. This helps them to sense warm-blooded animals nearby that might make good prey. The pupils of vipers' eyes are long, thin slits. Venomous snakes such as adders, rattlers, cottonmouths, and copperheads are all vipers.

The Gaboon viper of West and Central African forests and forest clearings is a much-feared viper. It is only about 3 feet 3 inches (1 meter) long, but it has large fangs that can be up to 1.5 inches (3.8 centimeters) long. Its splotchy brown color gives it good camouflage on the forest floor where it can hide in dead leaves and rocks. Its head is large, heavy, and shaped like an arrow. One reason its head is so big is that its venom sacs are so big. The Gaboon viper lies in wait for its prey without moving. When a small mammal comes close, the Gaboon viper strikes quickly.

The Gaboon viper has a very thick, heavy body. Its scales are keeled. That means they are thick and stick out from the body. When Gaboon vipers are frightened they hiss and even puff their bodies out to look larger and more dangerous. They may have as many as 60 live born babies at a time.

The western diamondback rattlesnake is also a viper that is greatly feared by people. It is one of the most dangerous snakes in North America because it can be aggressive if it is frightened. It has a large triangular-shaped head because of its large venom sacs.

The western diamondback rattlesnake has large fangs and blotchy skin that makes up a diamond-like pattern. Even with this distinctive (dis-TINK-tiv) pattern, diamondback rattlesnakes are sometimes hard to identify. They can be many different shades of brown, black, and gray to match the surface colors where they live. They grow a new rattle every time they shed an old skin. This may happen as often as 4 times a year. The rattle is a warning, and one that should be heeded. They are dangerous snakes! The western diamondback rattlesnake eats rats, mice, and even jackrabbits.

Snakes
FUNFACT:

Rattlesnake rattles are old scales that rattle together when shaken. Most rattlesnakes have only a few rattles because the old ones fall off.

This western diamondback rattlesnake is ready to strike.
Its fangs and triangular-shaped head hold large venom sacs.

Most snakes, like these black rat snakes, are harmless to people and do an excellent job of controlling pests such as rats and mice.

Snakes are some of the most amazing and misunderstood animals in the world. While it is true that some snakes are venomous, all snakes have an important job to do in the wild. Because they eat so many rats and mice, they help people by controlling these pests. Still, many people believe that "the only good snake is a dead snake." That is because many people do not know about snakes and are afraid of them. The more people learn about these fascinating animals, the more people will come to like and respect them, not fear them. No matter where snakes live, the most important way to protect them is to protect their homes.

One way to protect them and to protect yourself is to leave snakes alone. Most snakebites happen when people try to touch or bother a snake. So to be safe, respect and admire snakes from a distance.

My REPTILES Adventures

The date of my adventure: _____

The people who came with me: _____

_____

Where I went: _____

What reptiles I saw:

_____   _____

_____   _____

_____   _____

_____   _____

The date of my adventure: _____

The people who came with me: _____

_____

Where I went: _____

What reptiles I saw:

_____   _____

_____   _____

_____   _____

_____   _____

My REPTILES Adventures

The date of my adventure: _____

The people who came with me: _____

_____

Where I went: _____

What reptiles I saw:

_____   _____

_____   _____

_____   _____

_____   _____

The date of my adventure: _____

The people who came with me: _____

_____

Where I went: _____

What reptiles I saw:

_____   _____

_____   _____

_____   _____

_____   _____

Explore the Fascinating World of . . .

Turtles

TURTLES ARE fascinating animals that may be found in deserts, swamps, rain forests, rivers, streams, lakes, and even yards. Turtles are 1 of the 5 kinds of reptiles. Turtles are related to other reptiles, such as snakes, lizards, crocodiles, and alligators. They all belong to a group scientists call *Class Reptilia*.

Turtles are ancient animals that are like the other reptiles because of their scales and their cold-blooded bodies. That means their body temperature is the same as the air or water around them. Turtles are different from other reptiles because they have bony shells. Other reptiles do not.

A turtle's shell grows from its backbone. A turtle cannot climb out of its shell or live without its shell. As the turtle grows, its shell grows. A turtle cannot trade its shell for another one.

Turtles can pull their heads inside their hard shells for safety.

Green sea turtles use their flipperlike feet to swim great distances through the ocean.

Turtles, such as this Mississippi diamondback terrapin, like to sun themselves on a log over water. At any sign of danger they fall into the water—and safety.

There are 3 words used for animals that are turtles: turtle, tortoise (TOR-tiss), and terrapin (TERR-uh-pin). The name "turtle" is often given to turtles that spend most of their time in water. The name "tortoise" is often given to turtles that spend most of their time on land. The name "terrapin" is often given to water turtles that are eaten by people.

These names can be used in different ways and are sometimes confusing. Not all turtles live the way their name suggests. Some tortoises like to go swimming and even find animals and plants to eat in the water. Some turtles spend most of their time on land.

In this book, when talking about these animals in general, the word "turtle" will be used. Any reptile with a shell, no matter how it looks or how it lives, will be called a turtle. The words tortoise or terrapin will only be used when describing a certain type, or species (SPEE-sees), of tortoise or terrapin.

No one is sure where the word "turtle" comes from. It may have come from the Spanish word *tortuges*, (tour-TOO-gess). Spanish explorers used this word to describe turtles and turtle eggs that were an important food eaten by sailors on long journeys. The word "tortoise" may have come from the French word *tortisse* (tor-TESE). *Tortisse* is a word that describes a turtle's bent and crooked legs.

Scientists call all turtles *Chelonians* (kih-LOW-nee-unz). There are about 225 species of turtles in the world.

Turtles
FUNFACT:

All diamondback terrapin males have a dark stripe across the mouth that looks like a mustache.

Map turtle

Spiny turtle

Chilean tortoise

Soft-shelled turtle

Different types of turtles have different types of shells. Some are soft and leathery. Some are rounded. Some are ridged, and some are even spiky for protection.

Turtles can be found in most places in the world, from deserts to rain forests to oceans. They can live anywhere that the weather does not stay below freezing most of the time. They have shells that are made of 2 parts: upper and lower. The upper shell is called a carapace (KAIR-uh-pace). The lower shell is called a plastron (PLAS-tron). If you look at the inside of a carapace you can see the backbone and the way in which the rest of the shell grows from it.

The 2 shell parts are joined by supports that are like bridges. These are on both sides of the body and between the front legs and back legs. The shell is covered in bony plates and in layers of large, thick scales called skutes (SKOOTS). Turtle shells grow by becoming thicker and wider. If the turtle is injured (IN-jurd), or hurt, the shell can bleed.

To make the shell extra strong, the bony plates grow together in a zigzag pattern. Not all turtle shells are alike. Some turtles have hinged shells that close up like a box. Some turtles have soft, but tough, leatherlike shells.

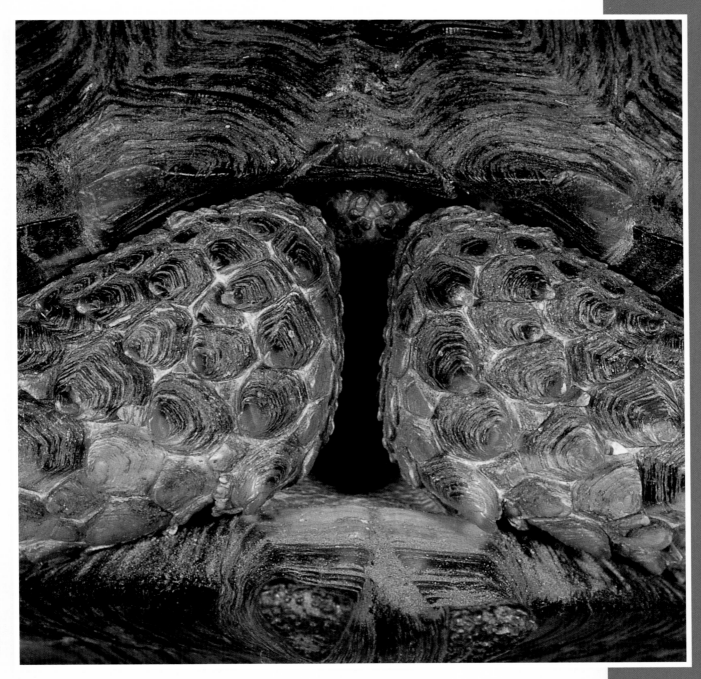

This Texas tortoise can protect all of its vital organs inside
of its shell. Here only the front feet are showing.

This giant tortoise eats the pads of a prickly pear cactus but spits out the spines of the plant.

All turtles use their sharp, horny jawbones to bite and pull food apart. Some turtles use their front feet to hold onto food as they eat. This makes it easier to tear the tough leaves and shoots. Some turtles hunt the animals they eat. Others just wait for a meal to come wandering by.

Different turtles have different diets.

Turtles that live on land usually eat plants. Some land turtles eat both plants and meat. Other turtles are mostly carnivores (KAR-nuh-vorz), or meat eaters. Some species have very special diets, such as the map turtle. This North American turtle has lines on its shell that look like roads on a map. It eats almost nothing but snails.

Turtles may eat different foods at different times of the year. During spring and summer many turtles may eat insects, worms, and other small animals. When the weather gets cooler and insects and worms are hard to find, they may switch to plants and berries. Turtles may not eat much food during the winter, or they may hibernate, or sleep through the winter without any food at all.

Many young turtles start life as meat eaters, especially while they are still growing. Often they switch to a plant diet as they grow older and need fewer calories (KAL-or-eez) and less protein. Turtles can go for a long time without eating at all, if they have eaten enough earlier to store fat in their bodies.

Young turtles need a lot of calcium (KAL-see-um) to strengthen their growing shells. Calcium is a mineral found in some plants and soils. To get enough calcium, many turtles eat sand or chalky soil. Some turtles also swallow small rocks or stones to help grind up the food in their stomachs.

Turtles
FUNFACT:

Turtles do not have teeth. Instead they have hard, bony jaw ridges that they use for eating.

Water is important to many kinds of turtles, but some tortoise species need very little water. The plants they eat give them the water they need. Other turtles wait until the rains come and water is easy to find. Then they drink a lot of water. The desert tortoise, a species from the American Southwest, can drink as much as 40 percent of its body weight in water in just 1 hour. All too soon the water from the desert rain will be gone.

Turtles
FUNFACT:

Sea turtles drink salt water then squeeze out the extra salt through special tear glands.

The desert tortoise drinks water that collects after a rain, or it may dig into the sand with its strong front feet in search of water underground.

Turtles that eat plants seem attracted to the colors yellow and red,
such as the red of the strawberry being eaten by this box turtle.

Animals explore the world around them using the senses of sight, hearing, taste, touch, and smell. The senses of sight, hearing, and smell are most important to turtles. Like snakes and lizards, turtles have an organ in the roof of their mouth that allows them to both taste and smell the air as they breathe it in. This organ is called a Jacobson's organ (JAY-cub-sunz OR-gen). It is named for the person who discovered its use.

The sense of smell helps male and female turtles find each other during mating season. Turtles can even smell underwater.

The sense of sight is important to turtles. Scientists have learned that turtles see in color. They use their color vision to help find food. They seem to like food that is either red or yellow. Sea turtles can see very well underwater. From underwater they even can see up onto land. Since sea turtles leave the water when it is time to lay eggs, this helps them to find their way. To protect their eyes from salt, wind, and dirt, sea turtles have heavy eyelids. This gives them a sleepy look.

Like snakes, turtles do not have ear openings. Instead they have round eardrums just below the skin on the head. These help turtles to feel vibrations (vie-BRAY-shuns) and hear very low sounds. Most turtles are quiet animals and do not vocalize, or make sounds. However, there are some species that do vocalize. Sea turtles may make wailing sounds when they are frightened or hurt. Some tortoise species make loud grunting or moaning sounds when they mate.

Turtles
FUNFACT:

Male common box turtles have red or orange eyes. Females have brown eyes.

Turtles have shells for defense. Turtle shells are tough and give good protection (pro-TEK-shun), but they can be broken. Box turtles have extra protection because they can close their shells up like a box, so that not even a curious dog or fox can bother them. This is because some parts of their shells are hinged. Most turtles cannot close their shells up like boxes and can only pull their legs and head inside for protection.

Shells give some turtles protection from fire. On the grasslands of Africa the grass becomes very dry in the summer. Lightning may cause grass fires that burn very quickly. Some species of turtles are safe inside their shells if the fire burns the dry grass quickly and moves on. If the fire lasts too long, the turtles will die.

Box turtles have hinged shells that close up like a box for protection.

Musk turtles are also called stinkpot turtles because of their strong and unpleasant smell.

Another type of protection is called camouflage (KAM-uh-flaj). Camouflage makes a turtle hard to see. Most turtles move slowly and are not brightly colored. Their shells may simply look like rocks sitting on the ground or partly buried in the ground. Turtles that hibernate have good protection because they usually dig down into the ground in a safe spot and are difficult to see.

Musk is another means of defense. It is a smelly, greasy oil that comes from glands in some animals. Musk turtles have these glands, and they give off a very strong smell. Common musk turtles have such a bad smell they also are known as stinkpot turtles. The strong smell may scare away other animals that might try to hurt the turtle. It also may warn other turtles of danger.

This common map turtle baby is tearing out of its soft, leathery egg.

All baby turtles are hatched from eggs. Some turtle eggs have hard shells, similar to chicken eggs. Some turtle eggs have tough, leathery shells. Some turtles lay only 1 or 2 eggs at a time. Sea turtles are different. Sea turtles may lay over 200 eggs at a time. The larger the female sea turtle, the more eggs she will lay.

Why do sea turtles need to lay so many eggs? Their eggs are buried in the sand at the edge of the ocean. Many things can happen to the eggs and the babies. Many of the babies will not survive and grow. The more eggs there are to begin with, the better the chance that some of them will live to be adults.

159

Female turtles search for a safe spot away from predators (PRED-uh-torz) to lay their eggs. They also look for a spot where the ground is soft. Most species use their back legs to dig a hole. Once the eggs are laid in the hole, the female covers up the nest and then leaves.

Temperature is important to turtle eggs. For many turtles, the babies will all be males if the temperature of the nest is cool. Females will all be hatched if the temperature of the nest is warm. No one knows why.

Many turtles never live long enough to hatch. Bacteria (bak-TEER-ee-uh) or mold may ruin the eggs. Predators such as coyotes or crocodiles may dig up the eggs. Many baby sea turtles are snatched up and eaten by sea gulls while they are trying to find their way to the ocean.

Turtles
FUNFACT:

Some turtle eggs are round and about the size and shape of a Ping-Pong ball. Others are shaped more like a large bean.

Huge female loggerhead sea turtles drag themselves onto the beach where they dig holes and lay as many as 200 eggs!

The map turtle's name comes from the fine lines on its neck, legs, and shell, which look like roads on a map.

Scientists study turtles of all kinds. They look at turtle shells, skeletons, and even blood vessels. There is still much to be learned about turtles.

Turtles belong to many different families and live in many different ways and places. Some turtles swim in the ocean, some crawl on desert sands, and some burrow underground. Nearly half of all turtles belong to one group or family. This group is called the family of pond and marsh turtles.

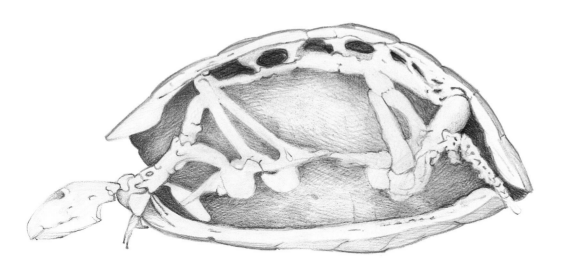

Turtle shells are a part of turtle skeletons and grow from the backbone.

Common box turtles belong to the pond and marsh family and can be found all over the eastern part of the United States. The shells of these turtles may be very dark and unmarked. Other shells may have a lot of yellow or tan spots, lines, and splotches. Their heads may have red or orange or yellow spots, or may be brick red. Box turtles spend most of their time on land, but they will go into water. They can even swim.

During the winter, box turtles hibernate by digging down into the ground. They do not wake up until it is warm again. Box turtles in the cold north may hibernate for 5 or 6 months of the year. In the warm south they may hibernate for only about 2 months of the year. In southern Florida, Texas, and in Mexico they may not hibernate at all.

Turtles
FUNFACT:

In Asia there is a type of box turtle that eats snakes.

Male box turtles have red eyes, but females, like this one, have brown eyes.

Box turtle shells close up like a box. This gives them good protection. It is very hard for a predator to hurt an adult box turtle inside of its shell. However, young box turtles may be eaten if they do not close up their shells quickly enough for protection. They also may be eaten if they are small enough to be swallowed whole or crunched into small pieces. Predators may include badgers, snakes, raccoons, crows, and other animals. Predators also eat box turtle eggs.

Box turtles are sometimes kept as pets. They do well if fed earthworms, dog food, tomatoes, lettuce, fruit, eggs, and bread. They also need water, warmth, and a place to hide.

Another common turtle of the pond and marsh family is the painted turtle. These small 5 to 7 inch (13 to 18 centimeter) turtles are found in many parts of North America. They are found as far north as Canada and as far south as Georgia and Louisiana in the United States.

Painted turtles get their name from their beautiful markings. They have green, red, and yellow lines on their necks and shells. Some of these lines of color are so fine they appear to have been painted on with a tiny paintbrush.

These hardy little turtles can withstand the cold winters of Canada and the much milder winters of the southern United States. In Canada they hibernate through the coldest weather. In the South they are active whenever the sun warms up the waters where they live, even in the middle of winter.

In the wild, painted turtles live in any slow moving body of water, from lakes and ponds to rivers and creeks. They especially like areas where there is soft mud at the bottom and lots of rocks and branches sticking up above the surface of the water. Painted turtles often are found clustered together on these rocks and branches, sunning themselves.

Painted turtles are often kept as pets.

It is easy to see how the painted turtle got its name—
from its beautiful colors and patterns.

The mata mata turtle rests in shallow water where its ridged shell looks more like a rock or a log than a turtle.

Outside of the pond and marsh family are many other, smaller families of turtles.

Mata mata turtles are some of the most unusual turtles in the world. They live in South America in shallow streams and rivers that come off the Amazon River. Mata mata turtle shells are flat with ragged edges. Mata matas also have ragged skin on their heads and necks. They do not move a lot and have a plant called algae (AL-jee) growing on their shells. This gives them good camouflage because it makes them look like a plant-covered rock. Mata matas sit very still on the bottom of a stream. They stretch their long necks so that their long, pointed noses stick out of the water. They use their noses like snorkels to breathe air.

To find food, mata matas move their necks slowly back and forth in the

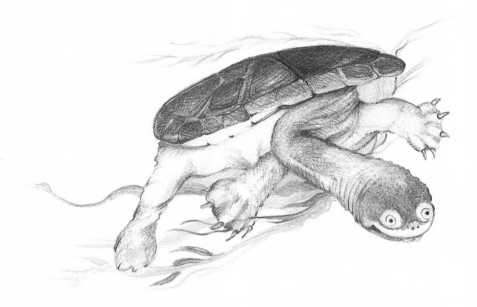

The Australian snake-necked turtle uses its long neck to reach out and catch fish as they swim by, much like a snake would strike its prey.

water. As fish swim by, mata matas suck water very quickly into their mouths. With the water, they also suck in the fish. Mata matas have very small eyes and poor vision. Scientists think that mata matas do not need good vision because they use their ears to feel the movement of water as fish swim by. This helps them to find and catch their food.

In Australia and South America there are turtles whose necks are so long they are called snake-necked turtles or side-necked turtles. Their necks can be as long as 12 inches (30 centimeters). Their necks are so long they cannot be completely tucked back inside the shell, so they are looped to the side in an "S" curve. These turtles spend almost all of their lives in rivers and only come on land to lay their eggs on the riverbanks. To warm themselves in the sun, they float at the surface of the water. Snake-necked turtles are nocturnal (nok-TURN-ul). That means they are active at night and sleep during the day.

Australian snake-necked turtles reach their long necks up to the water's surface to breathe.

Like mata mata turtles, snake-necked turtles can sit in shallow water and stretch their long necks to the surface for air. They can also move their long necks very quickly for catching fish to eat. In shallow water they may swim along slowly at the surface and stretch their necks down into the water in search of food. This is the way many ducks eat, and it is called dabbling.

Snapping turtles live in fresh water, which is water that is not salty. These turtles snap with their large, powerful jaws. Alligator snapping turtles are the largest of these turtles. The shell of a male can be 30 inches (75 centimeters) long. A male's head can be 10 inches (25 centimeters) across, and a large male can weigh over 200 pounds (90 kilograms).

The tiny red flap of skin on the snapping turtle's tongue acts as a fishing lure.

These large turtles do not move around very much. To catch the fish they eat, they use their special tongues as a lure (LOOR). They lay on the bottom of the river or pond with their mouths open. A worm-shaped piece of their tongue sticks out from the rest of the tongue and wiggles in the water. When hungry fish swim by, they see the wormlike tongue and try to grab it for a quick meal. The alligator snapping turtle snaps its powerful jaws shut and eats the fish. Crayfish, baby alligators, salamanders, snails, crabs, and even other turtles are caught this way. Alligator snapping turtles also eat acorns and fruit that fall into the water.

Snapping turtles may bury their bodies in the mud in shallow water with only their eyes and nostrils peeping above the water so they can see and breathe as they hide.

There are 7 kinds of sea turtles in the world. Sea turtles are turtles that live in the ocean. The green sea turtle lives in the Atlantic Ocean, the Pacific Ocean, and the Indian Ocean. It usually lives in warm water but sometimes it can be found in colder northern waters, too. It has a heart-shaped shell that may be as long as 5 feet (1.5 meters). A large green sea turtle may weigh 400 pounds (180 kilograms), but these larger turtles are becoming more and more rare.

Some people catch and kill green sea turtles for food, or so they can polish the shells to be sold as souvenirs (soo-ven-EARZ) to tourists. In many parts of the world it is illegal to hunt or sell sea turtles since they are an endangered (en-DANE-jurd) species. This means there are not many left in the world. Sadly, in some countries these laws are not enforced or are misunderstood, and the killing of sea turtles continues. In other parts of the world, people do not seem to care that sea turtles are endangered and prize them even more because they are so rare.

Green sea turtles are perfectly adapted to life in the ocean.
Without protection, all sea turtles could become extinct.

It takes about 20 years for a baby green sea turtle to reach adulthood.

Green sea turtles graze, or look for their food, in large seaweed beds. They eat algae, roots, leaves, and sea grasses. They also eat sponges, snails, jellyfish, and other small ocean animals. They are strong swimmers and may migrate as far as 625 miles (1,000 kilometers) every year between feeding places and nesting grounds.

Like all sea turtles, green sea turtles come onto land to lay their eggs. Females almost always return to the same stretch of beach to lay their eggs each nesting season. They usually nest at night and begin by slowly dragging their large bodies out of the water and up onto the beach. They sniff the sand looking for a nesting site and then dig a hole with their front flippers. About 100 eggs are laid in the nest. The female may return later to dig another nest and lay more eggs. The female may lay as many as 600 eggs in 1 nesting season. Many years later, after female babies have grown, they will somehow find their way back to the same beach where they began life. That is where they will lay their own eggs.

It takes between 50 and 90 days for green sea turtle eggs to hatch. This depends on the temperature of the sand.

The sand must also not become too wet or too dry. The eggs hatch all at once. All the baby turtles must dig together to free themselves from the nest. The babies often hatch after a rainfall and often at night. After they hatch, they must crawl into the ocean on their own.

In the ocean, the green sea turtle babies must find food right away and try to stay safe from predators. It may take as long as 20 years before these babies have grown enough to have babies of their own.

Turtles
FUNFACT:

The inside of a sea turtle's nose swells when it is underwater. This closes off the nose so water does not get in.

Soft-shelled turtles have soft but tough leathery shells and spend all of their lives in shallow fresh water.

Soft-shelled turtles are different from most other turtles. The body of a soft-shelled turtle, including the shell, is covered in a thick, leathery skin. This makes the shell seem softer than the shells of other turtles. The shell is also flatter than the shells of other turtles. Scientists believe these turtles have soft shells because they spend their entire lives in water. There are 22 species of soft-shelled turtles in the world.

Southern or Florida soft-shelled turtles live in lakes, rivers, swamps, marshes, and streams. They spend much of their day buried in the sand or mud at the bottom of the water. While underwater, much of their oxygen (AWK-zih-jin) comes directly from the water. It moves from the water through their leathery skin and into their bodies. In

Like soft-shelled turtles, leatherback sea turtles have soft, tough leathery shells, but they are much larger and live only in salt water.

this way soft-shelled turtles are specially suited to spend much of their lives underwater. They do not need to come to the top to breathe air very often. They also like to float at the surface of the water or bask in the sun on sandbars or riverbanks. Soft-shelled turtles eat mostly snails and insects and some fish. Females may be nearly twice as big as males with a carapace, or upper shell,

as long as 24 inches (61 centimeters).

The leatherback sea turtle also has a tough but soft leathery shell. It is not part of the family of soft-shelled turtles, but it looks and lives very much like soft-shelled turtles. One big difference is the type of water these turtles live in. Leatherback turtles live in salt water, in the ocean. Soft-shelled turtles live in fresh water.

Giant tortoises are some of the longest-living animals on earth and may live to be 150 years old.

Tortoises are those turtles that spend most of their lives on land. Most tortoises are found in tropical places where it never freezes. Many tortoises are large, live on islands, and can live for a long time without food. Sailors on long ocean voyages many years ago used to find island colonies of tortoises. They captured the tortoises and carried them onboard their ships for food to last for many months. Sometimes thousands of tortoises were taken from a single island in just 1 year. As a result, some species of tortoises became extinct (ex-TINKD). This means there are no longer any alive. Others became endangered.

Turtles
FUNFACT:

The smallest of all tortoises is the speckled tortoise. It is not quite 4 inches (10 centimeters) when it is fully grown.

The largest of all living tortoises are the Aldabra tortoises. They come from the Aldabra Islands in the Indian Ocean. They are the last of 18 species of tortoises that used to live on islands in the Indian Ocean. Male Aldabra tortoises have a shell that may be as long as 4 feet (122 centimeters). Males weigh as much as 550 pounds (248 kilograms). Females only weigh about 350 pounds (158 kilograms). Scientists believe these tortoises can live to be 150 years old.

Aldabra tortoises live mostly on the grasslands of their islands where they eat all sorts of plants. They even knock over small trees and bushes to get to the leafy parts. This gives the tortoises food and keeps the trees from growing too large. It also allows in more sunlight so that more grass will grow. That way there is always plant food of one kind or another for tortoises to eat.

Turtles
FUNFACT:

The largest turtles in the world are leatherback sea turtles. Large males can weigh 1,300 pounds (585 kilograms). That is more than twice as much as an Aldabra tortoise and about one-tenth the size of an elephant.

Gopher tortoises are important to the survival of many other animals in their habitat.

Gopher tortoises live in the southeastern part of the United States, mostly in Florida. They are unusual tortoises. Like gophers, they burrow underground. They spend much of their lives in the burrows they dig. These burrows are slanted down into the ground at an angle. They may be 10 feet (3 meters) deep and 35 feet (11 meters) long. Gopher tortoises leave their burrows in the middle of the day to find food, and then they return to the burrow.

The burrow makes a home not only for the gopher tortoise, but also for as many as 350 other animals. Most of these are worms, insects, snails, and other tiny creatures. Animals as large as frogs, toads, snakes, opossums, foxes, bobcats, burrowing owls, and bobwhite quail also find safety in the burrows. Without gopher tortoises to make burrows, these other animals would have a much harder time living in their dry, sandy homes. This makes gopher tortoises important to the survival of many other animals.

Terrapins are any kind of water turtle eaten by people. This is especially true of species found in the eastern and southern parts of the United States. Many years ago, terrapin meat was an important meat source for some American Indian tribes and for some settlers and pioneers in rural America. Today turtle meat is rarely eaten by people.

Diamondback (DIE-mond-bak) terrapins live in a large area, from Massachusetts in the northern United States to southern Mexico. They live on the coast, in spots where river water meets ocean water. These places are called estuaries (ESS-chew-air-eez). The water in estuaries is called brackish water, which means it is slightly salty. It is not as salty as seawater, but not as

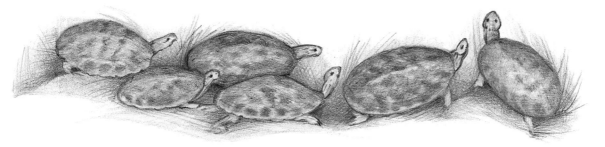

Diamondback terrapins often cluster together on a log to sun themselves.

fresh as fresh water.

Because they live over such a large area, there are about 7 groups of diamondback terrapins. Each group may look very different from the others. Some may have dark shells, some light shells. Some shells may have orange or yellow edges.

Diamondback terrapins have large, webbed feet for swimming. They spend most of their time in the water, but they usually stay close to the shore. These terrapins, and other turtles, like to climb out of the water and onto land to warm in the sun. Once on land, a whole group may climb on top of each other to try to find a perfect place in the sun. They close their eyes and rest and warm themselves. If one terrapin is frightened, it falls into the water. All of the others quickly follow with a splash.

About 100 years ago these beautiful terrapins were popular as food for people. So many of them were hunted that they nearly became extinct.

As the species has for millions of years, this green sea turtle crawls back into the ocean after coming ashore to lay eggs. Today, it will take help from people for all turtles to survive.

Turtles have been around for many millions of years, moving slowly but surely through the ages. Each species is an important part of its habitat.

Turtles are also important to people. They are an example of ancient reptiles for us to study, and they give us clues about the environment. Turtles do not survive well in places where the water and land are polluted. If turtles are present, it shows that the environment is healthy.

Turtles and their homes need the protection of people. With help, these reptiles will have a chance to live long into the future.

My REPTILES Adventures

The date of my adventure: _____

The people who came with me: _____

_____

Where I went: _____

What reptiles I saw:

_____   _____

_____   _____

_____   _____

_____   _____

The date of my adventure: _____

The people who came with me: _____

_____

Where I went: _____

What reptiles I saw:

_____   _____

_____   _____

_____   _____

_____   _____

Internet Sites

You can find out more interesting information about reptiles and lots of other wildlife by visiting these Internet sites.

http://animal.discovery.com	Animal Planet.com
www.tortoise.org	California Turtle and Tortoise Club
www.crocodilian.com	Crocodile Specialist Group
www.kidsplanet.org	Defenders of Wildlife
www.desertusa.com/animal.htm	Desert USA
www.yahooligans.com/content/animals/reptiles	eNature.com
www.enchantedlearning.com	Enchanted Learning.com
www.flmnh.ufl.edu/natsci/herpetology/crocs/crocpics.htm	Florida Museum of Natural History
www.cyclura.com	International Reptile Conservation Foundation
www.nationalgeographic.com/kids	National Geographic.com Kids
www.pbs.org/wnet/nature/reptiles	PBS Nature
www.sdnhm.org/exhibits/reptiles/index.html	San Diego Natural History Museum
www.scz.org/animals/home.html	Sedgwick County Zoo
www.vanaqua.org/education/aquafacts/crocodilians.html	Vancouver Aquarium
http://pelotes.jea.com/vensnake.htm	Venomous Snakes
www.kidsgowild.com	Wildlife Conservation Society
www.zoo.org/komodo/index.html	Woodland Park Zoo
www.worldalmanacforkids.com/explore/animals/snake.html	World Almanac for Kids Online

ALLIGATORS AND CROCODILES Index

LIZARDS Index

SNAKES Index

TURTLES Index

Our WILD™ WORLD SERIES

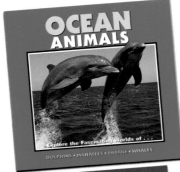  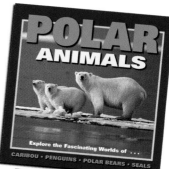

  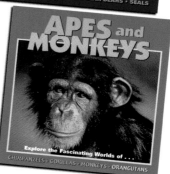

Look for these Big Books
in the Our Wild World Series: